Sugar

Upon My

LEMONS

Sugar Upon My Lemons

Published by The Conrad Press in the United Kingdom 2021

Tel: +44(0)1227 472 874
www.theconradpress.com
info@theconradpress.com

ISBN 978-1-913567-82-8

Copyright © Maria Conyers, 2021

The moral right of Maria Conyers to be identified as author of this work has been asserted in accordance with the Copyright, Designs and Patents Act 1988.

All rights reserved.

Printed and bound in Great Britain by Clays Ltd, Elcograf S.p.A

Typesetting and Cover Design by The Book Typesetters,
www.thebooktypesetters.com

The Conrad Press logo was designed by Maria Priestley.

Sugar

Upon My

LEMONS

A testament to love and loss
amidst the pandemic

Maria Conyers

I dedicate this to Graham's five children who loved him to their utmost without exception; Amanda, Cassandra, Jonathan, Natalie and Campbell.

I further dedicate this book to all those around the world who have lost a loved one in these tragic, dark days.

Friday 5 June 2020

Meeting you was fate, becoming your friend was a choice, but falling in love with you I had no control over.
Unknown

The moving finger writes; and, having writ, moves on: nor all thy piety nor wit shall lure it back to cancel half a line, nor all thy tears wash out a word of it.
Omar Khayyam

'This is the BBC at six o'clock…' I listened with horror and mounting sadness that Great Britain had passed the unimaginable forty thousand death marker from the virulent COVID-19 infection. Quite rightly the newscaster spoke of lives being cruelly cut short. Some of the deceased, bravely giving the ultimate sacrifice when caring for others, whether in hospital or social care. These unspeakable losses for the whole nation and individual families was akin to an unending, collective nightmare.

My loss was a drop in a tsunami of grief but it did not feel any less real or bring any comfort. In a vain attempt to distract my mind I chose to watch *Under the Tuscan Sun*, a chick flick movie which I thought would be cheerful enough to give me respite from the depth of the loneliness.

I felt as if I had been hollowed out. I was a numb husk of my former self. Life had lost all meaning. Only the love I had for my children forestalled a strong desire to join Parker.

Sitting on the loo was my favourite place to howl like the wounded animal I was. One could only hope that none of my neighbours could hear the sobs dragged from the depths of my soul. I longed to have just one more second with my dearest Parker. I would have given almost anything just to tell him one more time that I loved him and to hear his voice, perhaps to make a light joke of it as was his style.

This giant of a man felt deeply, but used humour as a defence. He was more likely to say, 'Ditto,' alluding to one of the films he loved.

However, having watched my chosen film I strolled into the kitchen. I knew my mind was being dragged back to memories of a holiday in Tuscany, of sunlight, wine-filled lunches in the local taverna with excellent, simple food, sitting in the Campo in Siena having an astronomical eight-course lunch and Parker savouring every mouthful, watching people running inside with the help of waiters to get out of a summer thunderstorm; loving the atmosphere created by the life of the bustling crowds; the architecture; every subtle thing that made up the magic of what Italy is.

My adoration of Italy pre-dated his, but I like to think I introduced him to a second love. It was so ironic then, that Italy was struggling so greatly with the horrors of the pandemic, as was the rest of humanity. I laid my head on the kitchen worktop and sobbed without restraint.

If this was a movie, there would be an on-screen image of memories swirling, pulling me back to happier times.

Year 1: 2010

Sweet Serendipity ... that unexpected meeting that changes your life.
Alexia

They say you should only write about something you truly know. This is not a novel, but it is a story, a truth that against all the odds, all hope and definitely all expectations, love can be found in the autumn of one's life. I hope this account both raises joy in peoples' hearts but it comes with a warning on the packet, to treat each second with your partner and loved ones as utterly special. Treasure them. Take nothing for granted because when you least expect it, those dreams, hopes and precious moments can be stolen from you.

My second bite of the cherry came to me when my heart was broken, and all trust in men had gone. A marriage of thirty-five years lay in the dust at my feet mocking me. The man I had loved since I was sixteen was having an affair with my best friend. Sorry for the cliché, but there it is.

For her it was a game, a bit of a joke. She told me it was, 'Just a bit of fun.' I, at least, credited my husband with his thinking that he was truly in love. Of course not. Once the excitement had gone, so was she, leaving my childhood sweetheart dazed and vulnerable.

Naturally, I had tried to deceive myself that our marriage could be saved. Thirty-five years could not be swatted away like a dead fly off one's collar. We paid a lot of money for therapy and exchanged lots of mutual hurt and misunderstandings.

We agreed we would have a good divorce, conscious that our children were watching us. We managed it and, to this day, we are amicable, even friendly, though our love burnt out a long time ago.

However, this book is not about infidelity, it is about a man whom I will call Parker. He was known to me before I knew about my husband's infidelity.

March 2010

Being shortsighted, I had advertised for a driver, as there was no way I could drive. To my astonishment over fifty people applied and I had a strong shortlist of eight. Actually, I did not immediately give Parker the job. He was married with three children and I never wanted to feel guilty about asking a driver to pick me up late at night, or take me on long journeys.

Parker, was larger than life in every way, with a military bearing. Upright and immaculately turned out in a suit and tie, with shoes so shiny you could see your face in them. A paunch like Father Christmas and a bristling moustache with twinkling green eyes that smiled a lot. He was an ex-copper at the Metropolitan Police and proud of it. Thirty-five years' service with a thousand tales to tell. Some embellished I am sure.

After the interview my secretary commented that I couldn't possibly offer him the job as all she'd heard was the two of us laughing together. It was true, he was a very funny man whose sense of humour chimed with mine. But I did not give him the job. I gave it to a professional chauffeur who proved to be pernickety and difficult about when he would and would not drive.

Sometime later, a chance meeting elicited the fact that Parker was still looking for work. It was a done deal, he got the job.

'Why,' I hear you ask,' Did you call him Parker?' In the early days if I casually said, 'Oh, I could just do with a coffee' he would smile and say, 'I just happen to have a flask in the boot. I believe in being prepared.'

It was the same with ice creams and cold drinks. I began to think he was secretly pulling my leg as he would call me Lady M whilst grinning at me. His ability to mimic Parker from the British TV soap *Thunderbirds* was amazing. The title so suited him and he was a skilled and professional driver.

He boasted that he had learnt to drive riot vans backwards at fifty miles an hour. On one occasion, when taking my friends and I to a gathering, he overtook a line of traffic and missed a lorry within a hairsbreadth (more of this later). We let out a collective groan of terror and relief but he remained cool and unperturbed.

In those early days I used to slip in and out of day dreams as I watched him drive. As the scenery flashed by, tales of Parker and his anti-terrorism expertise danced and amalgamated in my mind. This is a short story that his tales of daring-do and undercover work conjured up.

Go Bond Go

Karen shrugged on her briefcase as she walked out to the main reception area. A long day of interviews was over but it had been worth it. They had appointed a new company driver and he was due to start the following month.

James Bruce had been the successful applicant. A commanding six-foot-two, ex-policeman caught up in the rounds of early retirement who thought the future looked rosy, only to be hit by the credit crunch and national recession.

He immediately commanded respect, and Karen was in no doubt that his advanced motoring skills and evasive manoeuvres would stand them in good stead when either herself or her deputy managing director had to try and get to the airport in record-breaking time.

Karen was well-groomed, slim and attractive at thirty-five, so young to have reached the top of the tree and to own a computer technology software company. Indeed, the economic projection suggested the company would float shares on the open market within the next five years.

Karen had long brown hair, cascading in a well styled flowing mane. Her hair was her crowning glory, matched by her bright, intelligent blue eyes. Not only did she dazzle her male peers and colleagues with her stunning good looks but with the quickness of thought and the sheer ingenuity of some of her technological designs.

Material wealth is one thing, but it doesn't fill an aching void inside you. A healthy bank account cannot cuddle up to you in bed at night, nor make you coffee to reassure you in the wee hours when sleep is slow to come. Yes, she had got to the top of her profession, but at great personal cost. Now her body clock was ticking, though she was doing her best to ignore it. Karen felt that she hadn't done all this to be a stay-at-home mother. Nonetheless, during her limited time to walk round shops, she did find herself pausing at the baby section of Marks and Spencer or John Lewis to admire the frilly little dresses and tiny little bootees. Then with a self-conscious shake, she'd move on hurriedly to the household section.

James Bruce lived up to her initial assessment of him. He was courteous, punctual and resourceful. She laughingly referred to him as, Creighton. He always happened to have an umbrella in the boot, maybe drinking water or tissues. On the odd occasion, flasks of coffee, having noted with astuteness that she had been on the dash from one meeting to another all day.

When she had tried to make conversation with him about his work in the police force, he would merely reply that he had been involved in counter terrorism training and his role was mainly administrative. Karen accepted this with a half uninterested shrug.

Her young nephew of fifteen was far more interested to hear details about this. Goggle eyed he asked her, 'Did he know how to make bombs?' She laughed, amused at his earnest fascination, 'You've been watching too many *Die Hard* movies,' she said, 'Less television for you, wait till I speak to my sister.'

On the day that changed her life forever, there was no warning, no glimpse of anything unusual about to happen. They had just turned onto junction 29 of the Northbound

M25 when she noticed that her driver James had stiffened almost imperceptibly. He kept glancing in his rear-view mirror as he suddenly put his foot on the accelerator and took off at what felt like a hundred miles an hour. She jolted suddenly in the back seat and asked, 'James, what's going on?' 'Sorry Ms. Stewart, I will have to explain in a little while' and still his speed increased. He seemed heedless of the possibility of getting speeding tickets. She was having to hold on to the side of the car so as not to fall to one side. What the hell was going on?

'Mr. Bruce,' her voice had a cold clipped edge now, 'What do you think you are doing?' The reply he gave chilled the very marrow in her bones, 'I am trying to save your life!' 'Don't be ridiculous, what do you mean?' Karen snapped. 'Exactly that. I am trying to save your life. You thought you were recruiting a driver, that's fine, it fitted neatly with our plans, or we would have had to have found another excuse for my introduction to you and your company. I am actually an agent for MI6 and at this very moment you have people pursuing you who are intent on killing us both of us. So kindly sit back and let me concentrate on getting us the hell out of here.'

All of this he said without turning a hair or removing his eyes from the rear-view mirror and the road ahead. He was weaving frantically in and out of the cars, and at the first possible opportunity took the exit junction.

As they sped down country lanes he seemed to relax just a little. This could not be happening, this was fantastical, this was a lot of nonsense. Karen kept repeating in her brain. Who the heck would want to kill her? She was not of any interest to anyone. But then her mind seemed to flip back to six months earlier, the break-in at her apartment which could not be solved. It was put down to youths trying to take the opportunity to get any DVD equipment, expensive hardware et cetera.

There was another incident in the laboratory, where there had been an unexplained fire. In the end, the fire inspector and members of her team had to say they could only put it down to unfortunate misadventure with some of the equipment. But it still didn't answer this ridiculous question of why anyone would want to harm her.

As they turned the bend they saw two sinister looking black Mercedes coming up on either side, forming a pincer movement and blocking off their route. In a trice, James had switched the car in a handbrake turn and was speeding back the way they had come. Despite it being a one-way road, he was weaving in and out of cars expertly, banging on the horn as he went.

He called over his shoulder with more urgency in his voice, 'You'll find my guns under a false bottom in the glove compartment. Put your hand into the compartment, press the little screws to the left and the false bottom will shoot up.' Karen almost giggled, 'Are you having a joke at my expense Mr. Bruce?' 'Do as I am telling you now and stop asking stupid questions. I'll explain later.' Feeling more apprehensive now he said, 'And keep low for God's sake.'

She leant cautiously forward, keeping her head down and did as he asked. To her astonishment a panel quietly moved to one side and there were two large guns. She couldn't for the life of her be able to say what sort. They were just big and black and looked awful.

'Have you ever fired a gun?' he asked in a peremptory manner. She shot him a scornful look, that could have silenced many other colleagues, 'Oh yes,' she said in a clipped voice, 'Don't you know I do target practice every day just before I start my Pilates routine.' 'Now Ms. Stewart no need to be sarcastic. I just wondered. You are a thoroughly modern woman are you not?' She snorted, 'Now you are being condescending Mr. Bruce. It's not what I expect of an employee.' 'Yes, but I am not like any usual employee am I.'

Perhaps it was then that she really looked at him afresh. Somehow, she had never really noticed him as a person. She always treated her staff with respect but they were after all, staff. Now she saw that he had a toned and lean body, that he was trim but very muscular, that there would be no nonsense about him in any fight.

'But you still haven't explained why somebody is pursuing me,' Karen asked. 'We had a tip-off from a counter espionage agent. They want your new surveillance equipment that your company are currently developing.' 'And, so why does that make me a target?' 'Because with you out of the way, it could be much easier for them to make what seems to be a harmless takeover of your company a straightforward buy-out following your tragic accidental death, as you are the managing director and also the majority share-holder. They have to remove you to gain access to the prototype.' Karen sucked in her breath in sheer stunned bewilderment. He wasn't joking and this wasn't a game. She was in real danger.

Just then he swerved up the bank of the road they were travelling along and drove at high speed through an open farm gate, virtually taking half the hedge with them, across the field and came out onto another road going in the opposite direction.

'Well that's it for now,' he said, 'I think we've lost them and I will be getting other colleagues to pick up their trail. I have already sent a coded message.' 'Oh, pull the other one,' Karen said. 'What have you done? You've been driving all the time.' It was his turn to throw her a look. In his hand was a minute black box. He explained, 'Everything that we have been talking about has been fed directly back to other agents who are at this very moment in pursuit of your would-be assassins. This gadget is both a satellite navigation system, a homing device and a message output feed.'

After a moment, Karen realised that she was actually sitting rigid but inside, the core of her was shaking. She said, 'I think I need a drink or something.'

He turned off the lane and sped across the country roads until they came to a remote pub. He swung into the car park and replied, 'Yes perhaps we need a stiff one as opposed to a stiff corpse, if you get my meaning?' He winked.

She rolled her eyes and climbed stiffly out of the Audi Quattro, which was her preferred car. He took her elbow and masterfully steered her across the car park and into the pub. Not asking what she preferred to drink, James gave the barman an order for two double whiskeys. It was at this point that Karen realised that her trembling had spread to the whole of her and she was visibly shaking.

He sat down quietly beside her and said, 'We have to move to contingency Plan B.' 'What's that,' said Karen in a quaking voice. 'I have to take you to a safe house until my colleagues have apprehended the pursuers and we are assured that you are safe and this threat is eliminated once and for all. I don't think you fully realise the importance of the new prototype that you have been working on or its global significance. My superiors and I want to talk to you about that at a later stage. But right now, my orders are to escort you to a safe house and to guard you.'

She shook her head in disbelief, 'But what about all my meetings, my diary appointments. What explanation are we going to give?' 'It's already been given. I took the liberty of ringing a member of your staff saying that you have been taken unwell and that you were having a few days off, ordered by your GP. I explained that you would be out of action for a week, not to pass any phone calls, emails or other work-related matters through to you as the doctor has ordered. I said you would not be contactable on your mobile or home numbers and that when you were fully recovered you would contact somebody and return to work. Right, had the whiskey, feeling a lot calmer? Let's go.'

They stood up in unison, but as she got up to leave, Karen caught her foot in the stool. She wasn't paying complete attention and she lurched forward and fell heavily against him. He caught her quickly in his strong arms and looked down at her, flicking a strand of hair, that had fallen across her eyes, out of the way. 'Ms. Stewart, is this any way for a managing director to behave?' She looked up into his hazel eyes and wondered if there was just a hint of mockery in them. He really was an arrogant man, much more than she had originally felt. Then, of course, he was playing the job as the dutiful chauffeur, no more, no less. Now the tables had been turned. He was the one in charge and she, the underling, the person to be protected. It made every feminist hackle on her neck rise.

'I am perfectly all right,' she said, pushing him away with a small shove, 'I just caught my foot in the stool, that's all' and holding her head high she marched out into the car park.

The safe house was comfortable enough. It was an anonymous flat in an anonymous block in some anonymous town. After five hours of driving she didn't much care where she was. All she knew was that it was appropriately stocked with wine, spirits and food, both in the freezer and fridge, for every possible gastronomic eventuality. They believed in feeding their, what was the word, charges, victims, people? She was one of their people who had to be protected. She didn't like the feel of this very much.

Later that night, as she lay in bed, Karen suddenly gave way to all the pent-up stresses of that day. She found herself silently crying, scrunched up in a tight, foetal position. Crying from sheer loneliness, from exhaustion, from release of tension.

The door opened and a shaft of light spread across her bed. Instantly she stiffened and blew her nose. His voice came from the doorway, 'Are you alright Ms. Stewart?' After a moment's hesitation, 'Karen are you okay?' She replied, 'What do you expect, all of a sudden I am plunged into a world of guns, speeding cars and assassins. How do you expect me to be?'

He came in and sat down on the bed and held out a mug of tea with one for himself. 'I could hear you in my room.

Sorry, I didn't want to intrude but thought you might welcome a little distraction and conversation.'

As she drank her tea they fell into conversation. He didn't give much away. What Karen could tell, from the little he told her, was that he was single. All agents, she thought, must be. What else could an intelligence operative be? Who in their right mind would want to marry them?

He asked politely about her nephew. He seemed amused about the anecdote and said that perhaps one day he would give him a little talk about the dangers of fantasizing about building bombs. She laughed. He smiled directly into her blue eyes and said, 'You have a lovely laugh and it is lovely to see your smile. Has anyone told you, you have a beautiful smile?' To her annoyance, she found herself coloring and becoming hot.

He leaned forward and gently removed the empty mug, placing it with some decision on the bedside cabinet. Once he had put it down, he leaned forward and very gently tucked her hair behind her ear and planted a soft kiss on her cheek. Running his hand gently down the side of her neck, his forefinger just stopping at her neckline.

'God,' he said, 'You are so beautiful and you don't even know it. Your head is so full of company accounts and designs that you have never spent time knowing what a lovely woman you are. How come you are still alone after all these years?' Karen, was disconcerted, embarrassed and somewhat, turned on. 'I have been too busy to have any serious attachments,' she said, 'A couple of one-night stands but nothing more than that really. Like you say, a woman in my position can't be too careful, I guess.'

After a pause, he said very softly, 'There's being too careful and there's being a celibate nun, which is it?' Karen's flush deepened to rose red. 'I think that's rather insulting, don't you?' With a sudden movement, that she had no preparation for, he scooped her into his arms and began to kiss her passionately. First her eyelids and her mouth. Her own body responded to the hardness of his chest. Her heart rate increased and she felt herself yielding into his arms, falling back onto the bed lying next to him.

Covered by the warmth and masculine smell of his deodorant and manliness. God, she had forgotten that smell. It was so good and he was good too. Too good. She was losing herself, caught up in the moment of his strength and yet his sense of tenderness before he went further into their passionate caresses as he looked deep into her eyes and asked, 'Is this ok for you?' She silently answered, 'It's wonderful.'

Beyond that, there were no words, just the feeling of such closeness. A hanging together, each folding into one another. Karen, didn't know for sure, but she thought she had cried out in pure release of joy and she knew then that, for whatever reason, her life would never be the same again. She had never met a man like this before. Assured, quiet, tender and compassionate and resourceful. But he seemed to know her in a way she didn't even know herself. He had found a secret place within her that she had kept locked up. James had released the real woman in her, the yearning, wanting, needing a man in her life. She had truly been set free.

When, at last, they lay panting and hot side by side, James apologised and said, 'I hope you don't think I was taking advantage of your vulnerability?' Karen wordlessly shook her head. She knew in the depths of her soul that she had taken advantage of him equally. She had desired and wanted him but perhaps had never admitted it to herself until that moment in bed.

The silence lengthened between them and eventually James said in an unusually nervous voice, 'Look, I've got something to tell you, which might ultimately blow me out of the water and out of your life forever, or you might see the other side to it. I'll cut to the chase. I am not an agent working for MI6 and those two would-be pursuers were actually friends of mind. The guns in the glove compartment are fakes. I had to find a way to get through your defences and find a plausible reason to be alone with you. Yes, I guess, to try and find a way to seduce you because from the first moment you marched into that interview room, my heart nearly stopped in my chest and I knew I had to have you. Now go on, tell me what a heel and slug I am. Slap my face and chuck me out. Fire me, discipline me, court-martial me, report me to the police for fraudulent impersonation of an espionage agent. I don't give a damn! The truth you have to hear is that you have been like an ice maiden that has been locked up in your own ice cavern and I knew somebody had to get through to you. I came up with this crazy plan to take you to my safe house, to my safe place in my heart and, on one level, I guess I have blown the possibility of trust with you, but all I can say is I did it because I knew you were probably the only woman I would want in my life.'

The little bedside clock ticked away the minutes. Everything was still in the room. A shaft of moonlight came skimming through the window spreading a soft glow across the cream coloured carpet.

Karen was thinking rapidly, conflicting ambivalent thoughts. The bastard, to scare her like that. The liar, was he even an ex-cop? Then an internal smile riddled through her body and mind. If she was honest, the adrenalin rush of fear had been a real turn-on. Karen, gulped back a small giggle. If only her stuffy company board members could see her now.

After a moment's pause, Karen heard herself answer, 'Mr. Bruce, turn over please.' He rolled on his side and looked into her eyes. She leant forward, kissed him softly on the lips and said, 'You nearly scared me half to death today, you terrified me, and frightened me, by God you are a good actor but, more importantly,' she said leaning down under the sheets, 'There is another gun which I hope is in full working order that needs to be removed from its compartment.' She slid her hands under the sheet and with a small groan, he rolled onto his back as she drew nearer to him. There was nothing further to be said.

When Parker read this story, he threw back his head and roared with laughter. He gave me a huge wink telling me how much he fancied Karen, the heroin. I gave him a playful punch on the arm. Those early days were so hedonistic, filled with easy laughter.

Having shared my fantasy about Parker perhaps I need now to expand a little more clearly a picture of Parker's life as a metropolitan police officer. I jokingly teased him that one day I would write an account of his professional life entitled, *Confessions of a Local Bobby on the Beat.*

Parker trained at the police academy in Hendon and from the start felt privileged, and honoured, to be a serving police officer. He recalled, with some quiet dignity, his Passing Out ceremony at twenty years of age. Parker's tone and pitch changed as he recited word perfectly the oath he had taken on that day to serve his Queen and country and, if necessary, to lay down his life in the pursuit of justice.

Parker started off his career in the mid 1970s serving in King's Cross and Hackney police stations. These were some of the roughest areas in London at that time. He loved to be out amongst the people he served. Parker was eloquent and colourful in his accounts of his daily job. As well as upholding the law, he was strongly committed to the idea of community service. His many colourful stories were peppered with his brand of compassion, creative use and interpretation of the law.

Parker would settle back in his chair, fingers crossed over his expanding paunch, and would look into the mist of time and tell several favourite stories to any willing, but unwitting, audience that might be around. Parker was somewhat verbose in his reminiscences although loquacious and eloquent he could talk for hours recalling bygone days.

As a young policeman, one of his first roles was to take a group of physically and mentally disadvantaged adults for a much-needed holiday. One can imagine his dismay, as a green rookie police officer on arrival at the holiday destination, to discover that three of his colleagues had cried off, leaving just him and one other colleague to care for ten adults with special needs. Parker, with usual gusto, set to and spoke of the pleasure he derived from taking his young charges down to the beach and teaching them to swim.

There was, of course, a more serious side to his role in the police force. Parker's overriding duty was ensuring that law and order was maintained and to catch criminals. In many ways he saw life in black and white. There was little scope for grey. In his internal world things were either right or they were wrong. Therefore, he was clear about his role to apprehend anyone who would undermine the law.

On one particularly dark and foggy night, where visibility was very poor, he saw a dark shadow shimmying up a drainpipe. He leant against the wall and quietly waited for the thief to descend at which point he put his hand on the intruder's shoulder chiming in his usual booming autocratic tone, 'You're nicked!' Not surprisingly, his charge resisted arrest and aimed his bag of swag at Parker's helmet. Taken by surprise, he was momentarily thrown off balance but as a former forward prop in rugby his agility and strength soon outstripped the cat burglar and he was clamped in handcuffs. Such reminiscences were akin to listening to soap operas such as *Z-Cars* or *Dixon of Dock Green*.

On another occasion he was called to a house to assess a marital dispute which had got out of control and domestic violence was in full swing. Parker had no tolerance for any man who would not respect their wife or partner. He went to arrest the husband at which point the wife began attacking him saying, 'Get your dirty rotten hands off my husband it's none of your business.' The husband who had even greater girth and stature was having none of it so as Parker went to handcuff him the man grabbed hold of his wrought iron gate and slipped his hand over one end saying, 'Now what are you going to do pig?' As a sergeant on duty that night Parker winked at his young sidekick and said casually, 'I'll just show you.' Parker then nonchalantly proceeded to pull up a concrete post, with the rusty gate attached, straight out of the ground and dragged the amazed miscreant down the street dragging post and gate behind him, much to the amusement of bystanders and the young officers that had come upon the scene too late. The man bellowed all the way while being dragged by Parker to the local cop shop some half a mile away. In those days there were many more small and local police stations. This story he said, with a chuckle, went down in police legend.

Parker loved being called out to what he termed a bundle brawl in some city pub. He would be summoned on his walkie-talkie for assistance and dive straight in to bang heads together. He would elaborate these memories and say, 'Ah those were the days, when you could be a real copper.'

Parker admitted that by today's standards things were not always as politically correct as they should be. He played the law by the book and was in no doubt that it was his primary objective to protect vulnerable people and to enforce the law of the land. As a young officer in London he was called upon to see scenes that would frighten most of us. With sadness he regaled his rapt audience with stories of being called out to witness the sad and lonely death of some forgotten, lonely poor soul who had died a solitary death some weeks earlier. At these times his voice would be sad at how human beings could be so badly treated by society. His compassion was a great credit to him.

His moustache would twitch as he recalled one story after another. An incident he often repeated, as one of his party pieces, was the night when he saw a young adolescent smoking marijuana. He walked up to the lad and said, 'I have two choices here, either I can arrest you here and now and take you to the police station and we can both be bored by filling in lots of paperwork, or we can stroll over there and you can throw that reefer down the drain. The boy in question groaned, having just bought the smoke for fifty pounds for his dubious treat. Parker would not budge and just patiently waited while his young charge weighed up the pros and cons. Eventually he reluctantly walked to the drain and disposed of the offending article. At these times Parker would pontificate about the struggle of young people who had suffered from poor parenting and neglect. Often, he would be frowned upon by his peers for his compassion. In such circumstances he would send off young lives with wise words in the hope that they would try and change their ways.

As a senior sergeant he regularly volunteered to go visit young peoples' care homes, to talk with them, establishing relationship and rapport.

Parker was caught up in the thick of many great political upheaval and historic moments. He was there during the Brixton riots when a brick was hurled at his helmet, puncturing it and rendering him senseless for a period of time. No matter what, he had to go back into the melee. He recalled that on that day they had to battle for hours with the young protesters and, whether the constables were injured or not, they just had to get on with it; carrying on trying to quell the uprising.

Interestingly, and something which impressed me greatly, was the fact that he would not deride or judge the protestors actions preferring rather to strive to understand their frustrations, living in a society which discriminated against ethnic minorities. In the mid 1970s and 1980s British society was much more politically incorrect and discriminatory. Parker had many friends from diverse cultural backgrounds and he preferred to relate to people not to their colour or sexual orientation. I think that's why we became friends because I could see beneath his burly exterior that he had a true heart for serving the population as a whole. Obviously, such sentiments meshed well with my background in social care and mental health.

Parker was well aware that there were elements within the police force that were much more bigoted at that time. Repeatedly, he had been invited to join the masons, which he politely but definitely declined, and he felt this may have had a detrimental effect on his promotion prospects. We must bear in mind that we are talking about a very different mindset back then.

One rainy Friday, Parker interrupted yet another burglary and did not come off so well this time. The criminals, he was attempting to apprehend with another colleague, rounded on them and he was pushed forcibly over some concrete bollards. He spent many months lying on his back in great agony, notwithstanding two separate periods at the police rehabilitation centre where finally it was decided that he would never again be able to take the physical strain in front-line policing to lead his men into skirmishes where he might be further compromised.

Ultimately, this earlier back injury and his exemplary police record, lead to Parker's promotion, from a staff officer and acting inspector, to a deputy commissioner. He respected his senior officers and spoke with great fondness of the camaraderie and family spirit that prevailed during those years in the metropolitan police. He loved attending the police club in Epping and often took his very large family there for long extended boozy lunches. Parker never regretted a single second he spent in the force.

I would tease him about his shifts in the vice squad and asked him about unofficial perks when attending massage parlours in Soho. Surely, as a man, he would get turned on by such undercover work. He was genuinely horrified at such a notion. He accepted that there were corrupt police officers but he felt strongly that he had a professional job to do. He said, 'Once you've watched one porn movie you watched them all and if you have to sit through twenty hours believe you me there is no fun in it just tedium, but evidence gathering has to be done.' My teasing would fall on rather flat ground.

Parker was a man of high moral rectitude when it came to any official role. It's an aspect of him that I loved very much and we would talk about how standards have dropped in the last thirty years.

A slightly tangential example of this was when we would attend fine dining restaurants that would adhere to dress code. If Parker witnessed that diners wandered in wearing jeans or trainers and looking scruffy, he would question the management and enquire why they did not stick to their own policy. Why didn't they want to honour the obvious effort that they put into the cuisine on the front of house service. We would lament that, at the end of the day, profit seemed to govern all such decisions, and if millionaires chose to come in to a high-priced restaurant in jeans who are they to turn away good business. Yet we witnessed in a few years the disappearance of high-class restaurants which saddened us.

Professionally, Parker had one regret. He loved telling tales of his many court appearances and giving evidence at the Old Bailey. He would study legal reports as they came out and, on one occasion, he queried a decision made in court citing recent court evidence and rulings which the current presiding judge and the court clerk had clearly not had time to read up on. He felt, had circumstances been different, he would have loved to have qualified as a barrister.

I think that with Parker's many talents of dramatic interpretation and acting, it would have served him well if ever he had realised his dream of becoming a barrister. He loved the TV series *Rumpole of the Bailey* and in some ways his own idiosyncratic personality was as equally entertaining as his TV legal hero. However, by the time he'd reached this understanding in his professional development, he had a family with all the pressures of domestic life rendering it impossible for him to consider returning to university to study law.

I felt Parker had not fulfilled his obvious intelligent potential. We would discuss the merits of a diverse and wide-ranging genres in literature. Not surprisingly we shared a passion for whodunnit novels or television detective series. I think it quietly annoyed Parker when I could guess the murderer before him. I like to think that I extended his appreciation of good writing and introduced him to authors that he previously would not have read. Together we explored the merits of Austin Steinbach although we drew the line at Shakespeare. Sadly, at school Parker had been completely turned off to the potential delights in the beauty of Shakespearean language.

Returning to the current story at hand, the most unexpected chapter in my life was about to unfold. More dramatic and unexpected than any day dream story could be.

Within three months I learnt that Parker's wife had walked out on him and was having an affair herself. He was angered and equally hurt by her betrayal and the acrimonious divorce. It was natural that we would share our hurt, as friends do. Despite our friendship we knew there was a line not to be crossed and I definitely never thought I would.

Parker and I were both fifty-five. Within the year we were both on our own, nursing separate grief and pain with our respective worlds turned upside down.

All the children had been through a lot, struggling to come to terms in early adulthood with the bewildering and devastating breakdown of their secure family life. Not surprisingly, when Parker came on the scene, my daughter was watchful and mistrustful of everybody.

Looking back, with hindsight, there was absolutely nothing going on between Parker and myself. We were straight-forward employee and employer, though I was never a boss in the strictest sense of the word. I would happily buy him lunch or dinner.

October – December 2010

In late October I noticed that Parker was feeling down so to cheer him up I wrote him this poem called:

Some friends are forever

Sometimes in life you find a special friend
Someone who changes your life by being a part of it
Someone who makes you laugh until you can't stop
Someone who makes you believe that there really is good in the world
Someone who convinces you that there is an unlocked door just waiting for you to open it
When you are down and the world seems dark and empty, your forever friend lifts you up in spirit and makes that dark and empty world seem bright and full
Your forever friend gets you through the hard times, the sad times and the confusing times
If you turn and walk away, your forever friend turns and follows
If you lose your way, your forever friend guides you and cheers you on
If you find such a friend you feel happy and complete because you need not worry
If you have a forever friend for life, then forever has no end.

I also gave him a beautiful hand-painted replica of the Royal Opera House depicting his favourite opera, *Madame Butterfly*.

I sincerely thought we were just good workmates. Looking back, I think my daughter was absolutely right. The first day Parker came to our home her comment was, 'He fancies you, I caught him looking up your skirt as you went up the stairs.' I just laughed and said, 'Well that makes him a pretty normal man.' The joke was lost on her and she was instantly wanting to question whether I liked him. I now realise she was consumed with anxiety lest more turmoil would be heaped upon our fragile family group.

November 2010

Parker himself was always courteous and forever willing to help me in any possible way. He would literally carry my briefcase to work or if I was struggling to walk across a grassy field he would offer me his arm. He was taller than I and I felt extremely upheld by his strength.

In the months before I left for India he took me and my son to Cambridge. I told him of my studies of the poet Rupert Brooke who had lived in Grantchester for a time and met with the Bloomsbury set to have tea in the orchards at Grantchester.

I recall, it was a beautiful windswept late autumn morning with scudding clouds tinged with grey and edged with orange rose hues. Little waves whipped into miniature curls on top of the river which made a beautiful landscape.

Wistfully, I turned to him and said how much I'd love to walk across the field and stand by the riverbank, but with two false knees I felt my balance was a little precarious. His arm was extended and together with my son we walked in the sunlight across the field and I remember thinking what a very kind man, a real gentleman who demanded nothing from me but wanted to make me happy. I knew then that we had crossed the line and become close friends. I dared to show him a more vulnerable side but he never took advantage of it.

Parker was so kind to my son and included him all day long chatting about men stuff including sports and jeans. He was endlessly patient going shopping with him and his help that autumn day meant a lot to me.

Back in October 2010, I had bought a mobility scooter to navigate longer distances because both my knees had been replaced. I had very mild cerebral palsy in my lower limbs which left me with a slight limp.

Caught in an autumnal haze of pleasure in Cambridge, what struck me about Parker is that, unlike my first husband, he did not walk ahead and leave me to follow behind. Instead he stayed by my side and measured his long stride with my scooter talking to me and my son all the time. For the first time in years I really felt seen and included. I do not say this as a criticism of anyone, but it's so easy when you're fully mobile to forget and wander on ahead.

December 2010

A friend is someone who knows all about you and still loves you.
Elbert Hubbard

I was privileged to go to Mumbai to oversee a limb camp that my Rotary club had funded with the help of Rotary International. I had travelled down from Calcutta where I had given a lecture at the first women's therapy centre.

However, before all of this, I could sense that Parker was concerned about my welfare and safety. He was after all an ex-high-ranking police officer with specialist skills in security and anti-terrorism. He fretted if I would be all right with the drivers. Was the unknown chauffeur reliable?

It was the third time I have visited that beloved country. So many superlatives have been heaped upon that continent that I am left short for descriptive depth except to say that India is in my blood literally. I am the third generation to know of India's kaleidoscope of humanity striving amid misery, massive inequality and immense cultural joy and indomitable unflagging ingenuity and courage.

My parents were British Colonials who witnessed the dying of the British Raj imperialistic rule in 1947. They decided to make the United Kingdom their home. It is not surprising that they made this choice. They saw England as the mother country, a significant part of their heritage inculcated via their education in a very British system out in India. For example, my father had sat an Oxford entrance exam.

It is perhaps interesting to tell you that recently a nephew of mine had a DNA test which showed that twelve per cent had a link with the Province of Bihar where my parents' home was situated in Jamalpur. My father had long boasted that one of our ancestors had married a high cast Begum princess. As children we used to fall around laughing at such a notion.

To see three thousand human-beings travel hundreds of miles without arms or limbs, some of them crawling on bits of wood literally inches off the ground propelled by a bit of wood and a stick, was the most humbling and unforgettable experience.

An emaciated local man, of around the age of forty, kept coming back to our stand asking for a Jaipur hand to be fitted. Sadly, in rural areas, surgery can be crude and pragmatic. To fit a limb there has to be at least a couple of inches below the joint. My attention was caught by his urgent, non-verbal, gesticulations of entreaty standing in the queue repeatedly to get our attention. I asked one of our American volunteers, 'Should we not try to fit him with a new Jaipur arm?' After much fiddling, with padding and tape, the limb was in place. The gentleman began to cry uncontrollably as within seconds he had mastered his new prosthesis.

It made me think that in England we make a much bigger deal of such traumas. In India they take much more in their stride, wanting to get on with their lives. No long-term rehabilitation or intensive counselling.

He picked up a jug and kept miming tipping water on our heads. We looked at each other in puzzlement, to be told by the interpreter who had been hastily summoned, that this man had been a barber and now, with his new hand, he could earn a living to sustain himself and his family. I turned to a nearby wall and silently wept.

The business of that week left little time for self-reflection or self-pity. My heart was still broken at the loss of my husband. He had moved out into a flat on his own and was dating another woman.

At the end of the Mumbai visit, I'd arranged to travel round India and to end the trip in Kerala. We were indulging ourselves by sailing on a private small boat on Kerala's waterways. I remember standing on the edge of the doorway of the boat as it glided silently along the moonlit river. All I needed to do was to take one step off the ledge, and the river would submerge forever the depth of my pain and misery and my broken heart. Coming from a catholic background, I felt being divorced was a slur against me. Needless to say, I loved my children too much and came to my senses with a jolt admonishing myself for misplaced self-pity and melodrama.

There was little time to think of Parker other than a fleeting thought that I hoped he was all right.

Months later he was to tell me that whilst I was away he became aware of a deep yearning in the depths of his soul. He felt as if a part of him was missing. He missed our easy laughter and realised that he was falling in love with me.

Parker was simultaneously dismayed. What should he do? I was his employer and he relied on the income. If he risked declaring what he felt, he could lose his job. He later told me that, as he waited in the airport to greet us, his heart was pounding like a drum inside his massive chest. He was shaking all over like a teenage boy with anticipation.

He kept his feelings well-hidden contenting himself with a big smile and interesting questions as to our general welfare, whilst he collected our luggage.

Year 2: 2011

Loves secret sighs

There is nothing I would not do for those who are really my friends. I have no notion of loving people by halves, it is not my nature.
Jane Austen (Northanger Abbey)

It is true to say that we acknowledged together that we were good friends. We discovered that we had so much in common, our love of theatre, opera and soul music.

As friends, we took up ballroom dancing. Whilst in his arms, I began to experience joyous exhilaration in every atom of my being. This woman that walked with a limp suddenly found, in Parker's arms, that she could do the most daring Argentinian tango, bend backwards over his strong arm and be lifted high into the air as part of a practice swing routine, all for a wartime recreation ball to raise money for the rotary.

To be lifted high in the air straight as an arrow in that swing style to Glenn Miller's, 'In the Mood.' These memories bring back feelings of the immense exhilaration I felt in his arms. Dancing the waltz to the glorious strains of Strauss music, perfecting pull outs and reverse turns. I felt, for the first time in my life, the thrill of real movement as if I was flying. I had the soul of a dancer and all the while his gaze on my upturned face. Looking at him smiling down at me will live on forever in my heart. Little did I suspect then, the way my life was about to change forever.

Physiotherapist friends would come to watch and marvel at what I was achieving on the dance floor. Because of Parker I realised a childhood dream to dance and dance. We would practice for hours each week, determined to perfect each step.

We had been so lucky as a mutual friend, who was a Broadway choreographer and an experienced dance teacher, gave us private lessons. She tactfully realised that my right leg was the strongest and all routines lead off using my ability. At first, I could not dance for more than five minutes and he would laughingly pass me a glass of water.

By the end, we were dancing four times a week. I was literally a dance addict, a movement junkie but I think looking back, I just wanted to be held in his arms with my hand on his Ombre shirt as we gazed intently at each other. During an Argentine tango there was such a passion and fiery connection in that dance that I understood why so many dance couples become lovers.

I took Parker out for lunch to a Michelin star restaurant in Cambridge where I was attending a conference for the Society of Women Writers and Journalists. Parker loved his food and could eat his plate and finish off the scraps of everyone else's. He would think nothing of drinking fine wines and eating two desserts.

In every respect he was larger than life. His voice was several decibels louder than most people. His laughter, mixed with my irrepressible giggling, became contagious. We were often found uncontrollably convulsed with mirth, helplessly caught up in some private joke as dining onlookers would witness our joy.

Sometime later, however, I sensed he was very low and worried about his children and the continuing negotiations over his acrimonious divorce. On that particular day I had just finished my professional meeting in London so I took him to the Dorchester Hotel for afternoon tea. He was unconvinced that we would get a table with no reservation. I rang up, using my most imperious voice, announcing that I was expecting a table for tea.

Now what most of my closest family and friends know is that I have always played down my limitations. I have never thought of myself as disabled. In fact, I am extremely shortsighted. After going to the ladies, I walked to where I thought Parker was seated and saw a lone man sitting in a similar navy-blue suit, rather reminiscent to Richard Gere. I asked him why he had laid his coat on my chair not noticing his shocked and taken aback expression. I smiled at him sweetly and asked if he was enjoying himself. At that point, I realised the man opposite was a total stranger and I could make out Parker frantically gesticulating from another table with tears of laughter streaming down his face. With as much blushing and dignity as I could muster, I apologised and slipped quietly out of the seat and across the floor. In the years to come he loved telling people this tale and would embellish it dramatically.

Monday 24 January 2011

My eldest brother Michael was celebrating his seventieth birthday. To me it felt like a mad dash from India to Anglesey, despite the intervening weeks.

We were having a rare family reunion. Parker was driving me so I naturally invited him to stay as my guest, in a separate room of course. Although we were good friends, I did not want to give the wrong impression to either him or the rest of my family.

I had previously taken up singing as solace for my marital broken heart. To pay tribute to my brother on his birthday I sang 'Love Never Dies' from *The Phantom of the Opera*. The words of the song read like this:

Who knows when love begins
Who knows what makes it start
One day it's simply there
Alive inside your heart

It slips into your thoughts
It infiltrates your soul
It takes you by surprise
Then seizes full control

Try to deny it
And try to protest
But love won't let you go
Once you've been possessed

Love never dies
Love never falters
Once it has spoken
Love is yours.

The words seemed to touch several of my siblings as they knew of my heartbreak in the preceding eight months. Many a tear was surreptitiously wiped away. Parker leaned towards me, chinked champagne glasses and whispered, 'I have never heard you sing more beautifully.'

Parker fitted into my family as a hand into a velvet-glove. He was a rugby-playing man who loved introducing my younger brother to Glayva Whiskey Liqueur. Needless to say, they both finished the bottle and lived to regret it.

At the end of that first week one of my brothers, Brian, a man of few words, quietly asked Parker to look after me as I was struggling with being on my own. I think he guessed that Parker cared for me.

However, my dearest friend, and sister-in-law Helen, left me in no doubt as to what she thought. She challenged me, 'I know you're a bit shortsighted, but can't you see this man is in love with you?' She went on to tell me that when I had laughingly said I would marry him tomorrow if he won the lottery she heard him whisper, 'You do not have to wait until then.' Because I sincerely never believed another man would find me attractive, I did not even hear these words and at first pooh-poohed her suggestion, even though she told me he was secretly wanting to arrange a picnic on what was, in Wales, the equivalent to St Valentine's day in England.

The backdrop to all of these activities was my eldest daughter constantly asking me if we were just good friends and was anything going on, to which I truthfully answered no. I do not think she believed me, although then it was the truth.

In the freezing air of a frosty, sub-zero winter, Parker and I went on a solo trip. How we laughed like a pair of drunks on Bangor pier, when I mistakenly said, 'Oh hear the penguins cooing'! I had meant to say pigeons, of course. Parker had to sit down he had laughed so much.

Arm in arm, I could have strolled with him forever. Little did I know then that within six months my world would be shattered. We were so happy then, so caught up in our cocoon of joy. We fell in love.

We visited Portmeirion (where the TV series *The Prisoner* was filmed). It was a rainy Tuesday when the usually bustling famous village was mostly empty. We loved the philosophy of Sir Clough Williams-Ellis:

Cherish the past
Adorn the present
Construct the future.

Undoubtedly the Anglesey trip had raised questions in my mind. Looking back to my belated birthday, just after my return from India, all my friends went down with flu and I was likely to face the evening on my own. Parker stepped into the breach and offered to take me to one of his favourite restaurants.

The evening resounded with laughter, with jokes, talk of opera and novels (we were both avid readers and recommended books to each other). We liked to discuss them in detail for hours after reading, over large cups of coffee.

Holding his arm, we sauntered into the car park and he invited me to gaze up at the moon. I remember as we stood by the car, I was longing for him to bend down and kiss me and I thought how presumptuous. Later he told me how he longed to do just that but was afraid of my reaction.

Friday 18 March 2011

Only once in your life, I truly believe, you find someone who can completely turn your world around.
Bob Marley

One life is not enough for all this love.
Barbra Streisand (A Love Like Ours)

As Parker was driving me to a conference in Ilkley, the true state of affairs began to unravel. I told Parker that I was increasingly torn by my ex-husband's pleas to forgive him and take him back, yet at the same time I'd become aware of Parker's jokes of finding a little cottage where he could be my, 'Man of all works and driver,' and we could live together.

Summoning more courage, than I've ever possessed before, I asked him what these comments meant. We were sitting outside an Esso garage at the time and he asked me to hold that thought while he went in to pay. On his return his face was deadly serious and I feared that I had made a fool of myself. The atmosphere was taut and in the quiet stillness he looked down at my hand. He told me that he had fallen in love with me months ago. He said he couldn't believe his luck in finding a soulmate who shared so much of what he loved and had introduced him to so many new experiences including fine dining, cruising and extended literature.

I am not a psychoanalyst for nothing and was aware that in the first flush of infatuation one's brain becomes flooded with serotonin hence the wise old expression, blinded by love. We are, in fact, chemically blinded to our partner's faults in this jubilant wonderful head-spinning phase. I said as much to Parker wondering whether we were falling in love on a rebound.

As we drove down the M1 with sunlight playing all around us, he held my hand all the way and we played the Barbara Streisand album, *I Dreamed of You*. We were later to use this song at our wedding as it summed up the depth of our feeling.

We vowed to one another that we would live to be 105 so as to reach our golden anniversary remaining romantic to the very end. In that way we would outlive both our painful, previous marriages. Hope springs eternal. It is a mercy now in 2020 that none of us are privy to the future.

The next memory burns in my heart; our first official date. I felt like a young girl of fourteen. I told my colleague I was having dinner with Parker and hoped she wouldn't be offended. She merely winked and smiled.

We went to a Michelin star restaurant in Yorkshire called The Devonshire Arms, and afterwards I climbed the twenty steps to his bedroom. We just lay on top of the bed in each other's arms. I wore a pink silk dress and a shawl with a peacock design and he told me I was so beautiful. We did not attempt to make love but just gazed into each other's eyes and held each other close which felt like a rapturous interlude; stroking and caressing each other's bodies.

We were astonished that we had been blessed with such good fortune after years of grieving for failed marriages and our families torn apart and hurting.

Parker told me that whilst I was at the conference he went into a local parish church and thanked God for being given a second chance of love. He described feeling the hate and resentment he felt towards his first wife beginning to melt. It was by no means gone, but the realisation of a second chance of love, filled him with a sense of awe which he shared with the priest when they quietly sat down to talk.

Life is full of strange coincidences which Carl Gustav Jung called 'synchronicity.' When we had talked weeks earlier, we discovered the amazing fact that we had literally worked two doors away from each other when he was in charge of a police station in Barking many years before. I was working in social services and we were in our early twenties. We liked to fantasise of our paths crossing but, of course, we would not have noticed each other as we were both married to different partners. He laughingly told me that he had looked so different in his youth, so slim and so strong with all the rugby playing. As I recall and bring these memories to life, tears course down my face in both gratitude and sorrow.

All of you, who have been so horrifically and suddenly bereaved, will know how much one would give for five minutes to tell a loved one how much they really meant to you. The regret that you did not declare your love morning and night but rather, so often, turning off the light with an absent minded, complacent, 'Good night,' is haunting.

If only we realised at the time about these precious, precious possibilities of grasping each second of intimacy. Not letting the strain of modern living cloak the initial breathtaking ardour of those early days. We unconsciously allow ourselves to be seduced by the pressures and demands of work, family and domesticity that seems to make up everyday life in our modern world.

Year 3: 2012

Oh, what a tangled web we weave, when first we practice to deceive!
Sir Walter Scott, 1808

We were both concerned about the potential reaction of our five children. We did not want to deceive anyone but we were aware of how much they had all secretly suffered. We decided to try and keep things quiet for as long as possible; to let them get accustomed to the idea of us as a couple.

A period of espionage began. We naughtily invented distant friends, Gus and Julia, who had invited us to stay overnight in Sheringham, knowing that neither sets of children would know of these fictitious friends.

In fact, they were owners of a bed and breakfast, lovely people who made us feel so welcome. Parker had gleefully driven me down there one sunny afternoon saying he had a surprise. With a mischievous grin he would keep twitching at his moustache. He drove so quickly I could not read the road signs and I kept guessing where we might be going.

Parker, with a flourish and a smile, led me to an old-fashioned Victorian teashop, sadly now shut down as so many businesses are. The evening air was still and balmy as we strolled by the sea. We needed so much time together. I recall our rolling around with laughter clutching helplessly at each other as we giggled non-stop like a pair of hysterical schoolchildren on Sheringham seafront as the sun set over the darkening sea.

The reason for our mirth is lost in the sands of time but it was an example of how much joy we shared in those hedonistic days.

Our ruse was soon discovered. Parker had mistakenly packed a black lace basque he had bought me as a gift. However, this oversight became the stuff of legend as Nicola, his youngest, indignant daughter, with hands on hips waggling the offending article in front of him, commented that surely this, 'Skimpy thing,' couldn't belong to him as, 'It wouldn't fit round one leg!'

Parker kept a straight face and tried to appear innocent, confused at how it had got there. What a mystery! Nicola was having none of it. Needless to say, within days his three children had a family conference. They wanted to know what was going on.

After an urgent summit meeting of two, slightly naughty lovers, we agreed to come clean with our children. For one thing my daughter, Louise, was too clever and she had noticed signs long before we had, so we underwent the Nazi style interrogation of whether we were friends officially or not. It was becoming too much. I loved her and did not want to be caught up in deception so the game was up. It's true to say that they were not initially bowled over with joy.

Louise, my first born, had long since scathingly nicknamed Parker as, 'Beaver,' because she said he was, 'Fat and round with a smooth bald pate' which reminded her of a fat beaver. She meant it to be derogatory and insulting but within months this very term became a loving, affectionate joke. We would be out shopping and hear yelled across the road, 'Beaver, Beaver... it's me Louise.'

This giant of a man was the most loving and unselfish person I think I've ever met. He was always there for his three children and for my two children equally. He would drive to Kent at any hour of the night to take his own daughter papers or items she'd forgotten and needed. He acted as a chauffeur at 4 am to my daughter whenever she needed a lift.

When she had a prang in the car it was him she tearfully rang asking for help. He was there in a flash with a strong arm, a tissue and practical well-informed advice. Likewise, with my son, they became firm shopping buddies.

Oh, how he loved to reminisce about wonderful times with his precious children. Ariel, his eldest daughter, at twenty-three made him so proud when she achieved a first-class degree in horticulture.

What gave him support, as he struggled emotionally with his divorce, was the period when he went over to Highlands Park for three months tagging ancient trees. Parker treasured these special hours spent with Ariel eating sandwiches and chatting away in the beautiful grounds.

Year 4: 2013

Enjoy life today because yesterday is gone and tomorrow is never promised.
Author Unknown

As with all things in life there are periods when one's memories become like a kaleidoscope screen of possibilities. So much happens, so fast. Perhaps this period is less vivid as we were caught up in the hum drum of living and getting to work and managing our separate homes, making space for each other whenever possible.

It was a year I remember of beautiful skies, of long drives on what felt like endless summer evenings. We had a shared love of admiring beautiful orange and mauve tinted evening skies. It might sound silly to many people but we took great joy in witnessing sunsets together. We would stay up late and listen to Magic FM.

Because we had nowhere official to meet, trying to take our children's feelings into account and not encroach too much on their home life, at fifty-six we were looking for places to have a discreet cuddle, and I do mean cuddle! Driving down leafy country lanes we would try and spot remote laybys.

On one occasion, as the evenings were drawing in, and the air was tinged with the hint of winter chill, we were told by a kindly curator of a private garden that they never bothered to lock the gates at night as it was impossible to police the four-acre, deserted Victorian gardens. He winked at Parker and said how beautiful the summer house was. Perhaps it was obvious to him how much in love we were and that we needed some privacy. However, we never did go there after dark or fulfil the plan to take blankets and coffee and make love under the stars. Life had other plans for us.

May 2013

I now come to a very painful part of our story. I had organised a war time recreation ball at the end of April, where Parker played the part magnificently of the air raid warden. We had black out curtains, air raid sirens and everyone came dressed in 1940s costumes.

We had been practicing our ballroom dancing non-stop and were very excited at the idea of showing off our ability to waltz, fox trot and specifically to dance an exhibition tango during the dining interval.

At the same time, I was terrified as I was also due to sing Glen Miller's, 'Moonlight Serenade,' with a Glen Miller specialist orchestra and we had only rehearsed twice together. I can honestly say that whilst I sang it was an out-of-body experience as I was extremely nervous. I only have a two-minute video of our dancing together. Little did I know that within a week, this video would have a significance absolutely no one could have predicted.

On the 8th May I went in to hospital to have a right knee replacement. I had fallen previously when visiting Anglesey and it transpired that I had fractured my patella. However, I kept on walking and dancing, despite the increased pain, and I kept putting off the surgery date.

I wonder now if, unconsciously, I had a premonition or foreboding about this procedure with a new surgeon previously unknown to me. I can only give a layman's account of what happened following that surgery. I knew immediately something felt different from all the other knee replacements and surgery I had had in my life. My leg was extremely weak and I kept getting strange pains in my quadriceps. What I later learned was that my surgeon had snipped my outer thigh quadriceps, in his mind, to assist the function of my knee.

I will never forget the moment when I went to step down from my house and my entire leg gave way in sheer, unspeakable agony. Dear reader, you must believe that I am not accustomed to screaming or outbursts of melodrama. I imagine the whole town could hear my screams of agony as Parker, looking dazed and astonished, scooped me up into his arms, laid me gently in the car, and took me round to the physiotherapy clinic I owned.

They immediately sent me for an MRI scan which indicated that my central and medial quadriceps had ruptured. The bottom line was that my right leg, which had been the strongest leg you will recall from my dancing, was never again able to lift up my body. I had lost the vital twenty degrees that allowed me to stand strong and tall. To this day I have not been able to stand unaided or walk.

Overnight, I had become wheelchair dependent and went in to a physical state of shock and depression not believing what had happened to me. It was brought painfully to consciousness when I overheard the physiotherapists talking in the hydrotherapy pool after a session saying, 'She will never walk again, there is nothing left in her quadriceps, poor thing.' When I challenged the surgeon, he was reluctant to take any responsibility.

I, Parker and my family had to come to terms with a hugely changed lifestyle. For at least the next two years I tried to kid myself, in denial, that I would rehabilitate and walk again but more importantly almost dance again.

I tried everything. Specialist machines that held up my body weight while I practiced walking, cycling in rehab clinics to test if my nerve function in my leg was impaired or not. All sadly to no avail.

My heart was broken. I felt shattered and humiliated. I felt devastated and belittled that I could not walk beside Parker and wear the beautiful dresses he liked to buy for me. I literally felt less of a woman in a wheelchair.

I felt invisible, or patronized, by well-meaning strangers. People whispering, wondering if I had had a stroke, what was wrong with me. All conveyed to Parker, not to me.

My children were as shocked by all these events. Yet another tragedy for them to try and adjust to. Lifting me up if I fell in the shower and pushing me around in a wheelchair.

Because of all this, I decided to move in with Parker and allow them to have the space to be the unencumbered young adults they had a right to be.

The year passed in a blur of hope, determined rehabilitation and daily dashed hopes and dreams. Nightly I would dream that I could walk across a market place and run upstairs yelling, 'Look at me, it's all been a huge mistake.' I don't dream as often as I used to about that now.

What pulled me through these terrible months was the love of Parker and his total acceptance of me as I was. He kept reiterating I was still the beautiful women that could sit across the table and chat to him. That we would allow nothing to alter how we lived.

To prove his point, one day, he took me for a walk along the Essex way on my mobility scooter. Whilst three quarters of the adventure went well there were some undeniable hairy moments where unexpected tree routes and steps had to be creatively engineered. In these moments he was unflaggingly cheerful and positive, but in the depths of my heart I felt half a person.

However, I hadn't lost my feisty determination to be as healthy as I could, even if I couldn't walk. I attended a local gym, three times a week, and people would come up to me and say things like, 'Deep respect.' My trainer would laugh it off saying I was fitter than some of the thirty-year-old's who worked out. On one occasion an old friend came up and said in a sugary voice, dripping with condescension, 'Oh I think you are so wonderful, so brave' and from the depths of my soul the worm in me turned and I told her to, 'Fuck off' and stop patronising me. I was just trying to be like everyone else and be fit. Keith, my much-respected gym inspector, turned away to hide his smiles.

Parker took me to and from the gym, and all these rehabilitation centres without any complaint, turning his life around to support me.

Year 5: 2014

Things do not change, we change.
Henry David Thoreau

By this time, I had moved in with Parker and we had thought all ways round the struggles of immobility.

Now I must reveal a secret about Parker. He was an inveterate hoarder, although he would not admit it. When I first saw the house, my heart sank. The dining room was full of cardboard boxes and I remember being astonished that he kept the ashes of his beloved dog Lucy on a shelf above the buried, dining room table, that you could barely see for papers and all manner of detritus.

I had warned him before I moved in, and he had seen my home, that I was at the other end of the spectrum. I needed a home that was clean, tidy and interior designed to within an inch of its life. To give you an idea of the chasm between how we viewed the home, one of my previous homes had been voted one of the eighth most beautiful homes in the country and was featured in the glossy magazine *25 Beautiful Homes*.

I gave him fair warning that I am a yesterday person, everything had to be done now if not yesterday. I loved the fact that with his great ability for mimicry he would march round the house with a strong German accent, goose stepping and imitating Herr Hitler, making it quite clear who was the boss. In the end the children and I dissolved into laughter and I had to give up issuing imperious demands to strip the lounge wallpaper.

Within a year the house had been completely transformed. All boxes had been put in to storage. The kitchen was knocked into the dining room and a conservatory was added. In these areas all thresholds were removed and I had a nifty gadget in the kitchen, at the touch of a button, the sink and hob would rise up and down to suit any level of work, it was brilliant.

Initially when I was still in the denial phase I would try and climb his two flights of stairs thinking that eventually it would strengthen my legs, but by the twelfth step I was always very tired. My knees would sink to the ground. Parker and I devised a very clever way of getting me up the last eight steps. He would hold my trousers from behind and on the count of three gave me a little wedgy and uplift. We tried hard not to giggle but it worked. Eventually I came to my senses and we installed a stair lift.

I want to give praise and acknowledgement here to all our dear children who loved and accepted these changes without comment or complaint and tried in every way to make me feel comfortable about who I had become. I would scoot backwards round the house on an office chair trying to keep my core and quads constantly engaged, also burning up calories, an important thing for most of us women.

Parker and I still had romantic days in Cambridge. He would always admire and comment on the clothes I was wearing and how lovely I looked.

To ignorant friends who asked him on the quiet, 'Are you sure you know what you are taking on, things have changed now, Maria cannot walk,' he would stare at them coldly and reply that he knew exactly what he was taking on. Such comments hurt me deeply but I was not surprised by them. He later told me that what he really wanted to do at such moments, in his usual forthright manner, was to, 'Punch their lights out.'

There is, in society, still taboos, both conscious and unconscious discrimination, toward people who become different; who do not fit into the norm or the present-day pre-occupation with the body beautiful. If a disabled person should speak up or say, 'Don't be patronising and condescending,' the able-bodied person's defence is that they are over sensitive or have a chip on their shoulder.

I remember one occasion when we had visited Cambridge, on many a jaunt, and I had used a disabled badge to park outside in a designated place in front of a group of young men having a pint. One of them said, 'Lucky thing being able to park wherever she wants, it's all right for some people.' I calmly got out the car, mounted my scooter, drove over to them and smiled sweetly at the young man in question and said, 'I'll gladly do a deal with you, you can swap my legs and parking disc and I'll have back my so called normal, mobile life.' There was a stunned silence. All the other young men squirmed and started to remonstrate with him about his ignorance and apologised to me. I said there was no need, I merely wanted to make a point that I would give anything to be like them again.

What helped me through all of this was my job as a psychoanalyst and my ongoing work with patients, none of whom knew consciously that I was not mobile as they just saw me sitting in my chair as usual waiting for them.

What I have learned from life and thirty-five years as a therapist is that there is no such thing as normal. We all carry some disability. Some are injured on the inside, hidden and unseen by the rest of the world, but they are nevertheless limited and disadvantaged by struggles within their internal world.

Disability, as I have written about and lectured in the past, is not just a physical state but more a state of mind. You are as disabled or as enabled as you choose to be. We are all special, unique individuals and we have to make the best of whatever life throws at us.

This has never been truer than watching our nation, as it comes to terms with a pandemic wreaking havoc in the world. We will survive and come through this because as human beings we have a tenacity and optimism that can keep us going against all the odds.

Dear reader, please forgive a little conflation surrounding this year. Parker and I began to grow in our relationship and really understand the daily importance to try and adapt to each other's expectations. I think we had both been the driving force in our previous relationships. When two strong minded individuals get together, creating an emotional explosion, culminating in something of an immovable force, then there can be fireworks. Happily, we usually managed a mature compromise. Despite some rare moments of cross words and frayed tempers, harmony was soon re-established.

However, despite my love for Parker, he was no saint. The dishwasher had to be stacked his way and only his way. He was used to being the boss in his home. Then I came along with my own strong opinions.

It was an even more difficult transition for me. I had given up my marital home and had to fit in with a home that Parker had lived in for over thirty-five years.

He was marvellous to accept such huge architectural and interior design alterations in his family home. We would squabble over whose turn it was to create dinner. We were both keen cooks and rather touchingly wanted to create dishes for one another. However, we had one very important thing on our side, we were able to communicate and understand where such stresses emanated from. We were realistic about the struggle to make changes and live with another human being later in life. Sadly, our younger children might not have understood this period of transition and I guess from their perspective, and to their surprise, they saw two people in love squabbling.

We took immense joy in transforming Nicola's bedroom to mark her twenty-first birthday. She was away at University and we knew we had the time to transform her room using subterfuge and previous knowledge.

We bought new furniture and carpets and decorated her room with birds and butterflies and giraffes befitting a young woman's style. I placed a huge pink bow on the outside of her door and we were like two excited teenagers ourselves wanting her to go upstairs and see the outcome of our love for her. Nicola's screams of delight were all the reassurance we needed that we must have got most of it correct.

The rest of the year, and the next, was partly taken up with landscaping our back garden, which you can imagine had been trampled down and buried under the builders' rubble when the kitchen and conservatory were constructed.

The garden, once landscaped, was truly beautiful. I used my love of interior design to bring every nook and cranny up to the mark with eye-catching curios at every corner.

The existing oak coloured, wooden chalets were painted like a summer beach hut and a mountain stream was created down a natural hill. The theme was, largely speaking, romantic aided by the inclusion of a Victorian gate. The planting was done on a symmetrical basis. The plants mirrored raised beds of roses and lavender. Everything was accessible for me which was perhaps just as well because although Parker liked to boast that he loved gardening, I suspect he loved watching football on the TV far more. He was, however, the best person to sweep up the garden leaves and we would laugh together as we sat drinking tea and wine and talk about our respective strengths in the horticultural field.

That was our saving grace, the laughter between us, the jokes and teasing that I now believe was mistakenly interpreted by the children. They misunderstood our moments of light-hearted banter that was full of love.

My search and longing for effective rehabilitation had not stopped and I tried one so-called specialist after another, still determined that I would walk using crutches.

Unfortunately, whilst we were on holiday with my daughter Louise in Lanzarote, my right collar bone snapped in half because I was putting so much weight on my crutches at the time.

I was walking in the swimming pool with Parker and it took ten burly men to lift me out. We tried to take all of this in and philosophically accept the need for further surgery on my collar bone. I was determined that I would not be defined by these irritating limitations. So, the year moved on and we did as well.

We had of course talked of marriage and what the children would make of it and whether in fact we wanted to go down that road a second time. Needless to say, Parker saw the common-sense approach of being able to leave me half his pension in the event of his death, which, of course, we thought was decades away. Had we not promised each other to live to 105?

I was honest with him and said that I did not hold him to any expectation of marriage, now that things had changed. I did not want him to feel compelled to marry me out of a sense of gentlemanly honour, a code I knew he lived by both in the police force and in his private life. I told him that I was happy to release him from the pressure of marrying me and all that might entail in the long term. Parker would brush aside such discussions and say strongly that I was still the same, beautiful woman he'd fallen in love with.

As a compensation for our inability to dance we took up singing duets from musicals and light opera. Parker had a wonderful baritone voice and, like myself, had sung in choirs in his youth. We loved duets such as 'The Prayer' and 'It Had to be You.' Our musical taste was wide and eclectic. Parker did a wonderful rendition of 'Nessun Dorma.'

His ability to learn languages was clear and, much to my irritation, he quickly outstripped my ability to speak Italian. Whilst I had a broader knowledge of the language, his ability to mimic the correct intonation made me refer to him as a, 'Touché la bullshitter.'

I owned a villa in Calabria with stunning 360-degree views of the lake and the range of mountains. Parker fell in love with it and spent many a happy holiday with me and all the children at various times. His ability to drive abroad and cope in very powerless circumstances was simply amazing.

One summer, during a nightmare return journey down the mountain, which I will never forget as my poor daughter was being copiously ill in the back seat, the sat-nav mistakenly told us to turn up a mountain lane.

We were both quietly becoming more and more anxious as we noticed grass growing in the middle of this now tiny path and on the outer side a sheer drop of thousands of feet to the mountain valley below. The path became narrower and narrower and everything in the car was still and hushed, pulsating tension in the air. The strain on everyone was palpable. Finally, when there was virtually no road left, the lane literally petered out into the side of the mountain. Parker squeezed my hand which rested on his knee, a little habit of ours, and whispered, 'There is no room to turn around. There's nothing for it I will have to reverse all the way back down.' No-one spoke and inch by inch, with infinite care and skill, he, at last, brought the car to safety. Only the most skilled driver could have pulled this off saving all our lives. The advanced driving lessons he had done in the police force came to our rescue that day. This incident underpinned the fact that Parker was a man of very definite, quiet courage. If it were possible, I loved him all the more for this.

He was always ready to help with any of the children's requests. On one occasion my son, Cam, wanted to have what he called, 'Big bad-boy fireworks,' and invited round a close-knit group of seventeen-year old school friends on bonfire night.

Parker obligingly got the biggest fireworks in town. He set them off and all the boys, hid like cowards, positioning themselves behind a bench. They were happiest when they had sparklers in their hands and Parker and I smiled at each other thinking they were more like youngsters than half grown men. I am sure this will be vehemently denied by my son but it is a fun memory of mine.

It is a sad truth that when life brings trauma and change you find out who your friends are. After our divorces, and particularly when I was chained to a wheelchair, we saw the true colours of some of our friends. Many dropped us. There were no longer dinner party invitations. Some people were more forthright in that they just couldn't be bothered to deal with the hassle of someone in a wheelchair. This would incense Parker, whereas I was irritated but not unduly shocked as I had seen so much of this type of behaviour in my work within hospitals when patients became unwell.

I believe that young people today are more tolerant and open-minded in the main than our generation had been before. All our children and their friends were completely cool about holidaying with Parker and I. Great Britain has a very precious resource. The young people in this country cope with diversity and difference in a much more politically astute manner.

We have seen acts of true courage and selflessness in the youth of today during this pandemic. So many volunteered to help and I witnessed this amongst my five children.

We were both always arranging little trips for each other as a surprise. I took Parker to Hintlesham Hall for a much-needed spa retreat. However, in April 2014, I was at a very low ebb. Rehabilitation had come to a standstill and I was beginning to admit to him and myself that I might never actually walk again, not even on crutches.

Parker was having none of this and we had arranged to meet a former specialist physiotherapist in Richmond. He decided to combine this consultation with an impromptu surprise for me. He was always researching on the internet for ideas of things for us to do.

Parker found a wonderful hotel in Sussex called Ashdown Park, a beautiful Victorian mansion that was a former convent complete with a chapel, beautiful garden vistas and secret walled gardens.

As we wandered around, taking everything in, Parker ran up the stairs. There was a pause and he called down, 'Sweetheart if I help, can you manage up the stairs as I simply must show you this.' I was never one to turn down a challenge and using old technique and a crutch I somehow managed. What a joy awaited me.

Upstairs held the most sublime and totally unexpected sight. Within the chapel there was a stone vaulted reception area flanked at one end by the most beautiful stained-glass windows.

Parker sat beside me on the seat and looking deep into my eyes said, 'My darling now this is a place I can marry you in. I had no idea it was here but I know it is the place that we should be married.' I blinked back tears of happiness and whispered, 'Is that a proposal Mr. P?'

Now as I have previously told you I am unequivocally a woman of the moment. I was thinking that this marvellous venue must be booked up for years in advance. I suggested we talk to the wedding planner over afternoon tea.

The rest is history as they say. She told us that the following year's date, 20th March was available. This was, in fact, the date we had first declared love to each other five years earlier. We looked at each other and decided to arrange the wedding ceremony for the next year.

Parker laughingly told anyone, that would listen, later that it was like a train gathering speed and that before he knew it the reception and ceremony had been booked. We were invited to the following weekend's wedding fair. It felt as if it was meant to be.

It goes without saying that 2014 was a year of wedding planning. Parker happily threw himself into the planning with me. There was never a sense of it being my wedding it was our wedding in every way. We chose everything together, apart from the wedding dress that is.

I recall one night he was on the computer in the study whilst I was on my laptop as we went through playlist after playlist choosing music we wanted to have at our evening reception. We would play one track and discuss it in detail. Eventually I called out, 'Shall we have a cup of tea, it must be midnight.' Parker poked his head round the bedroom door and winking at me replied, 'What time do you think it really is?' I shrugged and said, '12.30?' He then laughingly revealed that it was, '5.30 am!' We'd been listening to music for hours on end. We were so happy that the time had passed by unnoticed.

Previously, Parker had taken me to a wonderful restaurant in Covent Garden where we had had a fantastic evening listening to international singer Colin Roy. We loved his voice which was smooth and reminiscent of Nat King Cole.

I came up with a brainwave and said I would write an email to him explaining that whilst I could not dance in the way we used to, I wondered if he could sing at our wedding.

Colin was simply marvellous. He sent us a CD of his recent music and then agreed to sing for us. In fact, he performed at least two hours longer than was officially allowed and he gave a golden edge to our very special day.

I was anxious as every bride about looking my best. I was no spring chicken and at times felt like an old rooster. I went into one renowned bridal gown establishment and the young shop attendant looked at me with a sneer on her face saying she doubted there were gowns or anything in the shop that would suit me. I felt so humiliated sat there on my mobility scooter that I simply turned around and, without argument, came out. I do not admire my lack of courage at that moment. I should have talked to her about being politically correct or empathetic polite alternatives that she could have employed. Thankfully this incident was a one-off.

I chose a dress of cream silk and lace requesting for it to be cut shorter, rather than full length, so I could not trip if I attempted to walk down the aisle on my crutches.

Parker even got involved in choosing the bridesmaids dresses. We were both in agreement about the colour and the style. My three bridesmaids, all my daughters, were still in their mid to late twenties. They were great supporters and we all had immense fun watching them trying on dress after dress.

Our children are the biggest blessing in our lives we knew it then and I know it now and always will do.

Parker was such a tease explaining to well-meaning strangers that we were getting married and that our five children were so excited. These poor souls would look bemused or shocked depending on their outlook in life and say, 'You've got five children and you're only just getting married?'

Parker would laugh at my bright red face and obvious embarrassment and told them, 'We've been living in sin for years!' I would protest and ask, 'Do you want everyone to think that?' Parker would simply laugh and tell me not to be so old-fashioned, that I was caught up in my childhood catholic up-bringing, which of course was spot-on. 'We're having a bit of fun' he would say. He loved the joke and his sense of humour never deserted him once, not even in the final days of his life.

Of course, in the preceding four years we gradually began to meet all his family and friends. He had a huge family of extended cousins and aunts and uncles as I did. Therefore, you can imagine, paring down a wedding guest list was like a military campaign and took a lot of careful thought.

Year 6: 2015

If I get married, I want to be very married.
Audrey Hepburn

I decided that, this time round, no expense would be spared as my first marriage had been a small impoverished affair. My first husband was a medical student and I had only just qualified as a teacher so there was little money for anything special but at that time we were very happy with our family wedding.

This time, as a mature woman, I wanted to have a hen party weekend with my closest friends who had known me for forty years or more. Louise, being my eldest daughter was, of course, my chief bridesmaid and gleefully arranged party games for the weekend.

I had done my own research and had booked a truly beautiful cottage in the Cotswolds. I arranged for a butler to attend, as well as a chef, so we would not have to do all the domestic chores. The wedding planner was baffled as to why I wanted a butler in a suit when most wanted a butler in the buff! I pointed out that I was a mature woman and found it a bit repugnant but, in the end, I capitulated with the laughing encouragement of my fellow hens.

He turned out to be a lovely young man who told us tales of how demanding his job could be with younger brides to be. He found our good humour, but restrained manner, something of a relief. He told us that young brides who got very drunk at their hen parties would disregard the rules and try and touch him up.

When he first entered the cottage the young butler asked where the bride was, looking meaningfully at my daughter, a beautiful tall leggy blonde in her late twenties being the obvious choice. With some embarrassment I raised my hand and said, 'It's me… I'm the bride to be.'

What fun we had that weekend. Parker went off shopping to look for matching ties to go with the bridesmaids' dresses and had a beer or two with his friends. He chose his brother and son to be his best men. My son and partners of our daughters were to be the ushers. Everybody was involved in this wedding.

Parker and I had written and chosen all the readings ourselves. It was agreed with the registrars that the formal part of the wedding would be done downstairs and that later in the vaulted reception area a dear friend and colleague, who was a priest, would bless our commitment of love. What could be more perfect.

Thursday 19 March 2015

You know you're in love when you can't fall asleep because reality is finally better than your dreams.
Dr. Seuss

We had a wedding rehearsal the evening before the big day. My closest friend and sister-in-law, Helen, along with my beloved brother, Michael, and Parker watched me walk up the aisle towards them to our chosen entrance music. They gently voiced their concerns about my falling in front of everyone in my wedding dress. They were concerned that it would ruin the day for me. I admired their honesty and tact and knew they were right.

As much as I wanted to walk to my dear, forever friend, Parker on my own two feet, I knew that this time I had been beaten. One of my dearest friends, Diane, said, 'No problem, give me the hem of your wedding dress and the hems of the bridesmaids dresses, once shortened, and I will use the material to decorate your mobility scooter to look like a wedding carriage.' What a magnificent job she did.

Another friend made our wedding cakes and to the puzzlement of most guests made a small cake for Parker complete with a little beaver on top wearing a policeman's hat. Of course, only the children knew the significance.

Saturday 20 March 2015
Our Wedding Day

I've dreamed of you
Always feeling you
Were there
And all my life
I have searched for you
Everywhere
Songwriters: Callaway / Undsat Lovland

The big day had arrived with scudding grey clouds which could not dampen the anticipation and excitement for all concerned. Strangely I felt very calm and quietly got dressed in the bridal suite along with my bridesmaids. While my hair was being done we drank champagne. I gathered from Parker later on that he had been involved in welcoming all the guests. Of course, it was all right for his outfit to be seen!

In that beautiful setting we made our vows and chose specific readings. We had both spent hours surfing the net and libraries that found words to match the feelings in our hearts. Parker chose the first reading which was a quote from Bob Marley:

Only once in your life, I truly believe, you find someone who can completely turn your world around. You tell them things that you've never shared with another soul and they absorb everything you say and actually want to hear more. You share hopes for the future, dreams that will never come true, goals that were never achieved and the many disappointments life has thrown at you. When something wonderful happens, you can't wait to tell them about it, knowing they will share in your excitement. They are not embarrassed to cry with you when you are hurting or laugh with you when you make a fool of yourself. Never do they hurt your feelings or make you feel like you are not good enough, but rather they build you up and show you the things about yourself that make you special and even beautiful. There is never any pressure, jealousy or competition but only a quiet calmness when they are around. You can be yourself and not worry about what they will think of you because they love you for who you are. The things that seem insignificant to most people such as a note, song or walk become invaluable treasures kept safe in your heart to cherish forever. Memories of your childhood come back and are so clear and vivid; it's like being young again. Colours seem brighter and more brilliant. Laughter seems part of daily life where before it was infrequent or didn't exist at all. A phone call or two, during the day, helps to get you through a long day's work and always brings a smile to your face. In their presence, there's no need for continuous conversation, but you find you're quite content in just having them nearby. Things that never interested you before become fascinating because you know they are important to this person who is so special to you. You think of this person on every occasion and in everything you do. Simple things bring them to mind like a pale blue sky, gentle wind or even a storm cloud on the horizon. You open your heart knowing that there's a chance it may be broken one day and in opening your heart you experience a love and joy that you never dreamed possible. You find that being vulnerable is the only way to allow your heart to feel true pleasure that's so real it scares you. You find strength in knowing you have a true friend and possibly a soulmate who will remain loyal to the end. Life seems completely different, exciting and worthwhile. Your only hope and security is in knowing that they are a part of your life.

Then came the moment for us, charged with the deepest significance, the wedding vows we had composed ourselves after hours of discussion. We had both written separate vows then joined them into one, a united prayer of commitment which our dearest friend, priest and psychoanalyst, Chris, read out. A hush descended on the congregation as if they too knew the heartfelt depth of what was being said:

Our conjoined wedding vows:

Our marriage declaration to each other in your presence is this.

That we will remember always the qualities that attracted us to each other when we first met and how we felt as our feelings of attraction turned into respect, admiration and finally, love.

That we will work hard to turn our feelings of love into acts of love so that nothing and no person can divide us.

That we will always have kind and loving hearts that are quick to ask for forgiveness when it is needed.

That our love might grow to hear all things, believe all things, hope for all things and endure all things.

We will stand together facing the world and in so doing form a circle of love that gathers in dear family and friends.

We place our marriage in each other's hands and trust that our love increases and overflows beyond anything we can yet imagine.

If only I could share the surprise video that my clever daughter had arranged, secretly filming using several mobile phones around the room. This was delivered to Parker and I a year later on our first wedding anniversary. How tears of joy streamed down our faces as we witnessed again that awesome, wonderfully happy, enchanting day.

As we left the wedding ceremony a brilliant blue sky and bright sunshine met our astonished gaze. It was as if the sunshine had come out to compliment us. It felt like a day in June.

There were heart-felt speeches. By far the most memorable one of Parker and myself was when our five children stood up and planned a surprise display of their own. Ariel, Parker's eldest daughter, spoke on behalf of her two siblings and herself alluding to the joy we had after all the suffering.

My dear Louise had written me a letter which she read out to the assembled party:

Dear Mum

I write this on the eve of your wedding, full of excitement for what tomorrow will bring. I know you will look beautiful and

I will be so proud to walk down the aisle with you as your maid of honour. I'm sure I won't be able to stop smiling all day.

When you and Parker sat me down in the kitchen last year to tell me the news, my heart was full of happiness for you both. I remember it so well. We've all been through a lot and I have prayed for your happiness.

I'm so glad God brought you and Parker together and that he and his children are in our lives. I wish you and Parker a lifetime of happiness, love and laughter as you both so truly deserve.

Here's to your adventures together… I love you both. Love always, Louise xx

Everyone clapped and cheered and we were visibly shaken and moved by the love and support of this conjoined family that called each other brother and sister. This was the true icing on the cake and a blessing from on high that they could all get on so well.

My six-foot-two, elder brother Colin, always very supportive and loving, told me that he had just finished wiping away his tears from the wedding ceremony and then had to pull out his tissues again when all the children had finished their speeches.

You might be wondering how we managed the first dance. A lot of thought had gone into this moment. I had brought a beautician's chair that was raised up to its tallest level and with my highest high heels on I used this to perform the waltz with Parker.

Nothing daunted us as we danced around the floor to the strains of 'You Make Me Feel Brand New' by The Stylistics. In fact, we danced all night amongst our children and friends, twirling for hours and hours.

I am sure that every bride and groom say that their wedding is the best, as they are naturally biased. However, without exception, every guest, including Colin Roy, said they'd never been to a wedding like it.

I think we were very blessed by the lovely registrars who were so very warm and gracious in allowing us to have so many readings and songs and the service taking far longer than was normally allowed. This day will live in my heart forever.

Colin Roy sang for us until 1.30 am. In the end we wearily climbed the stairs to the wedding suite. My two brothers and Parker carried me up the stairs. What a beautiful room to spend so little time in. We were literally shattered with the emotional intensity of the day and all the dancing.

In hindsight, one mistake we made was in booking a flight for the next morning so it made breakfast with our loved ones too rushed. We later regretted that we could not spend the whole day with them at this lovely hotel.

However, wedding conventions observed, bouquets flung, after secretly telling one of my brothers to position Louise in line to catch it, we left for our honeymoon, a cruise in the Caribbean and Mexico.

We treated ourselves to an upgraded cabin with butler and private club. All the other members there were multimillionaires and I'm sure they looked at us with much curiosity. They tried to engage us in conversation to discover a background inroad. We did not own a house in Palm Springs but, of course,

I could say I had a villa in Italy which left them all wondering.

A week on from the day of our wedding we were dancing the tango in the wonderful deliciously warm waters of Haiti in a private lagoon and island. Parker suddenly became distressed. Looking down at his hand he exclaimed, 'Oh my God I've lost my wonderful wedding ring. How could I be so stupid to wear it when I was in the water and I've been using sun tan cream.'

We were, of course, dismayed but we were overwhelmed by the kindness of strangers. About forty people got off the beach came in the water and spent hours trying to find Parker's wedding ring for us.

Back on the ship we were met with many enquiries and words of comfort. Parker had to be pulled out of the water. He was so determined to keep looking and so very distressed to have lost it. I tried to cuddle away his distress and tell him we could buy another and it would be blessed like the first one but I could tell he felt absolutely miserable about it.

We did not let it spoil our honeymoon too much and later on I bought him a replacement. It could never be the same as the former because this had been chosen in Florence on the Bridge of Sighs. We had had it engraved with the words, 'One ring, two hearts beat as one.' This is the first time that I have revealed this to anyone but I feel in sharing it I pay tribute to the joy and love we had in composing it. To some it might seem corny and stupid but it meant something to us. The rest of the honeymoon passed by with memorable and unforgettable adventures.

We went on excursions which included swimming with

dolphins and manatees. I was more concerned about the welfare of the animals not living up to the experiences I'd had in Florida some ten years earlier, where the dolphins had been meticulously cared for and not overworked.

We found the heat in Thailand overwhelming and I was not particularly bothered about visiting Phuket. It was not the sort of place that appealed to us.

In the evening we would have fun, pretending to be interested in buying the Faberge egg, costing a mere £75,000! We would be hunted around the ship by the jeweler with a gleam in his eye as he felt confident he had potential customers in us. How wrong could anyone be!

Ironically, we met him two years later on another cruise when his eyes lit up and he offered us champagne in the Bulgari shop thinking once again we were going to buy a big piece of diamond jewellery. Parker just teased him and played along considering it to be a bit of harmless fun.

I've missed something out, something hugely significant. I've moved from the wedding to the honeymoon. Did you wonder? I have not told you about the formal proposal Parker made to me. It was so romantic and uniquely suited him, but this is not a talent show where everything is revealed, no holds barred.

Although I have shared a lot that seems acceptable to me and to aid your understanding of what led up to the final curtain and its meaning for all of us but I think: *True eloquence consists of saying all that should be, not all that could be said (Francois de La Rochefoucauld).*

You might also be wondering if I'm going to share with you about our wedding night? This is definitely not an episode from the film *Fifty Shades of Grey*. However, I do have a funny story to tell you about that particular book. Now seems as good a time as any.

Parker and I had been out and about on holiday and I had arranged a surprise visit to Salzburg to celebrate the fiftieth anniversary of the film *The Sound of Music*. There was to be a special reception which included meeting members of the Von-Trapp family and original cast, though sadly not Julie Andrews or Christopher Plummer.

The story was reenacted in the famous riding school where the film shot the famous choir competition at the end of the movie. It was all incredibly atmospheric.

After that special weekend, I'd finished reading all my books and in desperation wandered into WH Smith's. I read the back cover of *Fifty Shades of Grey* and thought it sounded intriguing. Three pages in and I was bored. I did not take to the style or content. I saw Parker had a new novel tucked into the seat pocket, an interesting Whodunnit.

I innocently enquired of him if we could swap books. He absentmindedly nodded as he was dozing. When he came to read it the next day, in a coffee shop, to his amazement he was surrounded by a gaggle of women fascinated that a man should be reading this book. He told all his friends that he was literally a, 'Babe magnet' and that they should buy a copy. He joked that he would carry around this book with him everywhere but in truth he told me it was just not for him.

In our respective roles we had probably seen and heard everything that humanity could reveal. We were not shocked but merely not interested. Despite this, for a joke, Parker carried the book around for many months to come telling me of the ladies that he'd been accosted by.

April 2015

The biggest joy, following our wedding, was undoubtedly the birth of our first grandson, Thomas. From the beginning he was a heart-meltingly, beautiful child in every way. As he grew older he clearly adored his grandfather who talked to him in Donald Duck speak. Thomas would giggle unstoppably as they played with the dinosaurs who, of course, had serious conversations with each other.

I should tell you, my reader, that Parker was potentially a fantastic actor. As a qualified instructor he was called into schools on many occasions to act out some role which fitted into the curriculum for the education of the children.

On one occasion, he played the role of a banana eating, gorilla. His young audience believed that he was one of the last talking gorillas on earth. He explored the question of conservation of wildlife with them and loved throwing the children bananas from a huge basket by his side and bellowing like King Kong.

On another occasion, he played the part of *Widow Twankey*. I witnessed him dressed up in costume which was an unbelievable sight. On show where his big hairy legs in stockings and hiking boots all topped off with a fuzzy wig and several layers of a voluminous dress. If anyone could pull off such a ridiculous appearance, it was Parker.

On another occasion we once went to a recreation production of the sitcom television, *Allo Allo* which focused on the French resistance in the second world war. I can honestly tell you that he could act the part better than the actors on stage and proceeded to do so to the amusement of the waitresses and other diners.

Eventually, the actors themselves invited him upon the stage. Parker gave an impromptu solo performance of about five roles. He played directly to the audience and lapped up all of the attention.

He loved telling stories of his life in the police force and people loved listening to them. I often said he should write them down and we would write a book called *Confessions of a London Copper*. Sadly, we never quite got around to it.

Saturday 1 August 2015
Family Outing

Dear reader, here is where I break with conventional tradition. On the 8th August 2020, Parker's three children asked to come and visit our home where they had last seen their father. So very hard for them and we laughed and cried over the long bittersweet weekend as we began to sort out what effects from their Dad's life they would like to cherish. I asked them, 'What memories do you think we should gather in about Dad's life?' This then, is some of their memories, which jogged mine.

It was decided that we needed a family outing in August. A chance to catch up after the wedding and the honeymoon hype had all died down. Parker's family were all committed animal lovers and, to my inward dismay, they chose Colchester Zoo.

If I tell you that they could collectively stand in awe and amazement, for up to an hour looking at cheetahs and lions, pelicans or penguins, you may understand my absolute boredom. My attention span was about two seconds per enclosure partly because, half of the time, I couldn't see the animals!

It takes me back to another funny story. Parker had arranged a Mother's Day surprise for me with my son Cam, whilst my daughter was at University. We went to Port Lympne Safari Park where they specialise in the rearing and conservation of silver back gorillas.

We were standing looking into the enclosure and after a few minutes I turned to Parker and Cam and asked, 'What is that mad gorilla doing tossing hay round on the end of a fork?' At which point everyone in the crowd, who had been in earshot of my comment, started to laugh. It was in fact the zoo keeper and I said, 'Well he should wear something bright so he could stand out more clearly,' whereas Parker, bent double, guffawing with mirth, managed to splutter, 'It's not a he, it's a she... God your eyesight is so bad.' I fell back against the cage laughing too, joining in the fun.

Cam who has always had a mischievous side to his nature kept pointing to trees or buckets and saying, 'What do you think of that gorilla?' I never lived it down.

The day had its tender moments as we had not officially come out. Every time Cam wandered away, Parker would drag me behind a rose bush or hedge; he kissed me ardently and it was delicious.

Back to Colchester Zoo. The hours dragged as I stoically tried to stick a grin on my face and look interested and fascinated. Parker, however, was not fooled. In the end, I gave up the pretence, plugged in my earphones and went around the zoo for the rest of the day listening to an audio book which was far more gripping. I think the children have just about forgiven me.

Year 7: 2016

The greatest legacy we can leave our children is happy memories.
Author Unknown

One of the highlights of this year was a collective holiday, staying at two villas, with all of our children and grandson. It was like a military operation getting all our children and their partners to take time off work in July and agreeing a date.

At the airport I felt like a dazed shepherd. Trying to ensure we had herded everyone together was no mean task. In the end we let the flock scatter and hope we'd all end up at the same departure gate in time. Trust Cam to get carried away shopping and have to run for it, much to my agitation. I do not like airports, they are a necessary evil.

Parker and I had financed the villas and had agreed we would take the children out for two special family meals. We had also invited his widowed sister to join us on this escapade.

At a rather up-market restaurant, I tried to fool the manager that all ten children and the two-year old baby in the pram was mine. He looked shocked and kept glancing at me until the penny dropped that I was too old to birth a two-year old. The children were in fits of giggles as Parker and I hammed it up throughout the meal. He was on top form. He loved playing mine host.

This man had a particular charisma and charm. He ordered port but, not satisfied with a tiny glass, he asked the manager to put three bottles on the table; after we'd already consumed a small vineyard of wine.

In the balmy moonlight we all struggled along the quiet lane, back to the site where the small villas were. The children had rushed on ahead and we were content to amble along the dusty lane with Parker's sister.

When we drew level with our villa we were surprised to see the children all lined up like the Von Trapp family. They individually wanted to thank us for the holiday and the meal. The gesture of their respect and gratitude was touching and has stayed with me until this day.

Parker lived life to the full with a gusto, spontaneity and optimism rarely seen. One of his favourite sayings whilst sitting in the sunshine, usually with a glass of wine, was, 'This and two thousand a week, I'd be set for life.' Half an hour later he would repeat this mantra but the sum had gone up to, 'Three thousand.' By the end of the evening, or weekend, it might be up to, 'Twenty thousand.' He just loved larking around.

However, Parker and I did have a serious dream. As mentioned earlier, I was a rotarian who believed in service before self. Parker was also extremely charitable and we seriously informed the children that should we ever win on the lottery, they should be in no doubt that most of it would go to The Magic Foundation.

We would have long and serious discussions about how we would help friends and family, never telling anyone about our win. Sadly, we never won. It is a dream still to be fulfilled.

The second major highlight of the year came about, as usual, because I had one of my mad brainwaves to hold an afternoon, grand savoy-style, afternoon tea party in our newly designed garden and summerhouse.

We hosted twenty-five people to a sit-down tea party complete with fine bone china, choice of tea and cakes, scones and fancies. The day was warm and balmy. We lit candles all around the garden and sat out until 11.00 pm. Parker and I went from table to table, talking to all our guests, beloved family and friends.

We had intended to have a second, repeat afternoon but before we could do this, events overtook us and we decided to move to Derbyshire.

Year 8: 2017

*When you do the things in the present that you can see,
you are shaping the future that you are yet to see.*
Idowu Koyenikan

I trawled through my little grey cells to see what memories would rise up through the mists of time for this year. One particular week stands out, highlighted as a golden, special period for Parker, myself and Cam, my son.

As I may have told you, Parker had a keen interest in the Western Front and had literally walked the whole line and was a member of the Western Front Association.

He planned a week away in France and Belgium as a birthday gift for Cam and took us to Ypres Thiepval Anglo-French Cemetery. As we were on our way I shared with Cam my love of the first world war poets Siegfried Sassoon, Wilfred Owen and Rupert Brooke.

What was notable was that, at the beginning of the week, Cam excitedly talked about wanting to find a German hat or a mortar shell case. He had seen one in Parker's lounge.

As the week drew on and Parker's wise and gentle explanation of the suffering of millions of young men, both German and English, one subtly saw Cam's attitude changing. He would stroll across poppy strewn fields with Parker to special, little known grave sites and on the last day I sneaked back to see what Cam had written in a remembrance book. He said he was grateful for the sacrifice that boys, younger than him, had given their lives so we could live in freedom and democracy. He never again made jokes about what he might collect as a souvenir but stood straight with his head respectfully bowed as, 'The Last Post' was played on a bugle at the cenotaph in Ypres while the sun set.

I think this week, more than anything else previously, cemented a bond between Cam and Parker. It was a shared emotional journey. A wise, older man acting as a guide and mentor to a budding young man.

The rest of the year was typified by feverish activity to get the house looking ever more polished to place on the market, alongside visiting major retirement villages around the country to suss out where we actually wanted to put down our roots for the next few decades. How sublime is ignorance. To not be able to see into the future was a blessing.

We had many a free weekend with dinner and wine included. We were assured it came out of the sales teams' budget, so we didn't feel too guilty. We would seriously inspect a lot of potential properties and we gradually made a short-list. We saw most of Britain in this way. It's a wonder we didn't bump in to the Faberge' egg man!

Parker had always loved the Peak District since he'd been there at the age of eighteen on a police training course. He had visited with his children every year and had spent many a week on his own as a serious walker in the Peak National Park. It was a done deal.

Whilst we were courting, he took great delight in arranging two separate weekends to show me, as best as he could with my limited ability, the places that had captured his heart, the stunning views and valleys that were imprinted on his soul.

He knew the Peak District and all its pubs and inns better than most Derbyshire born men. He was once invited to train to be a mountain rescue member in his earlier, fitter years which he decided would not fit well with his police career, so he reluctantly declined.

Eventually we found the perfect apartment for our semi-retirement. Dudley Court was the name of the village and it was renowned in the area as it was once used as a boys private boarding school.

Rumour had it that the school was closed overnight when some Japanese investors bought it out with a view to building on the extensive land. Their dreams were thwarted as, understandably, the local council took a dim view of such blatant disregard to the conservation area that Dudley Court was placed in.

The children were asked to pack up and leave immediately and when the investors found it sometime later, to their astonishment, the school was left much as it was on the day the children left. School books had been left open and beds left askew. It felt like a Marie Celeste school.

But I was more interested in the future than in the past. A new beginning, a chance of making new friends and a retirement fit for a king and queen.

My husband was a keen walker and knew all the trails and hidden secrets surrounding the local pubs in the entire district. He was gleeful about our move and this was infectious.

Despite my reservations, we moved into Dudley Court and started a new life. In my innocence I was to learn exactly what sort of new life it was. The plan was that he would drive me back to Brentwood each week to my clinic and he would work, part-time, as a trainer.

Furthermore, he took on the role of the most fantastic Father Christmas for a local acting agency. Parker was made for the role. His enormous girth and pot belly made him the archetypal Father Christmas. All he needed was the suit and hat.

I remember our grandson, aged three by then, along with my twenty-two-year old son, both spellbound and racing from one grotto to another. It was hard to discern who was the real kid out of the two. Cam would have sat on Parker's lap, if he could have done.

Obviously, this Father Christmas had very special information about Thomas. He seemed to know all about him in fact. Thomas, for his part, was speechless with wonder and awe.

An important moment for Parker, I knew, was the day he and his beloved elder son visited Wembley Arena. What shall we call it… The Temple of Football. Jay had bought the tickets for his father. What fun they had. I could tell the way they recounted their day in minute detail. Days like this between father and child are to be treasured and savoured. If only we could put them in a magical jar, undo the stopper and relive that day again when dark times befall us.

The year had come to an end, with the impending knowledge that we would soon be moving to Derbyshire to begin our new life.

Parker assured me that there would still be trips to Covent Garden and the Royal Opera house, theatre land and fine dining. I was, after all, an honorary city girl at heart. I'd long been a member of a prestigious private ladies' club in London and did not want to feel that, despite Derbyshire's beauty, our cultural interests would suffer.

One of Parker's compensatory dreams was to arrange a tour of all the stately homes that had actually been featured in the BBC version of *Pride and Prejudice*. Surely you will remember the scene when Colin Firth emerged out of the pool in his wet shirt. We never did realise this dream in Parker's lifetime.

The house was packed up and we were all but ready to leave. However, Parker had noticed his right leg had swollen up and had sores on it. We wondered if he had been bitten by something. Eventually he saw experts who diagnosed cellulitis.

On moving day all the removal men descended on our house like a swarm of locusts. Parker was in hospital having multiple tests which revealed that he required major heart surgery and replacement of his aortic valve.

Planning for the move had been stressful, made more so by our children's general unhappiness that we were leaving the town where we had lived for forty years. All of them had loved being able to call in and see us at the drop of a hat.

Louise, my eldest, was the most vociferous, pointing out obvious pitfalls. How where we ever to be local grandparents if we lived three hours' drive away; that we were too young to go and live in a, 'Grannie village,' and what if we became ill so far away. Her fears proved to be prophetic.

We tried to make the counter-argument that we were moving partly to ensure that none of them would be burdened with having to care for us as we grew older. I had seen the strain this had placed on intergenerational families and did not want this for my children.

It was decided we were moving but had we been informed one week earlier what was to befall Parker medically, we would never have gone.

Year 9: 27 March 2018

One should always be aware that after sunshine there is inevitably storms to come.
Maria Conyers

Poor Parker, stunned by the news of his impending heart surgery, still had a house to tidy up after the removal men had departed with gigantic lorries loaded for the long journey down to Derbyshire. The law stipulated that they had to pack on one day, drive down the next and had to unload in so many hours.

It was a beautiful Spring morning as we drove with excitement in our hearts to start a new life in a beautiful ground floor apartment within a five-star retirement village complete with indoor swimming pool, sauna, bistro and fine dining formal restaurant.

We were given the now familiar complimentary suite for a further one night. Imagine our shock then when an irate removal man said that the completion had not come through from an eight-party chain of buyers and sellers and they would either unload our furniture onto the pavement or take it back to Brentwood!

Fortunately, the management of the village were more humane and knew that the money transfers were merely a matter of time and let us move into our new home.

Within six weeks, Parker had been sent for further tests as he casually mentioned to his previous GP that he had been passing blood. Jay, his eldest son, was summoned to be with him as they told him they had found a tumour in his bowel and that further scans would be necessary.

We were all in shock. How could this be happening and why? But worse was yet to come. The local hospital called Parker and I in together and initially said that he had metastatic cancer in his lungs, liver, bowel and abdomen. They said how sorry they were.

Within two weeks they telephoned us in Derbyshire when all my six brothers and sisters had arrived to lovingly give support. During lunch an unexpected call came from the hospital. They felt the scans had been misinterpreted and that the primary was only in the bowel and surgery might be used.

Luck was not on our side because despite our initial joy, the colorectal surgeons were told that Parker would first need his pending heart surgery. By the time he had recovered from this, although he had made a phenomenally fast recovery from the ten-hour ordeal, the tumour had spread and had migrated. So, in the end, the first scan was perhaps not too wrong. But I digress into the medical history.

We still had life to live in Derbyshire and in the early days, whilst all this surgery was still to come, Parker and I made hay while the sun shone. One memory that will stay with us forever is when we took my daughter Louise and her partner on a picnic along one of the accessible trails in Derbyshire.

We walked to the highest viaduct in the country and along the way passed through pastures and valleys most beautiful; all enjoying the wildlife and country scenes as we passed by. Parker announced that this picnic was to be our signature offering with a traditional wicker hamper that I had bought him as a gift to cheer him up and demonstrate that whilst we had life we must live it. Strawberries, champagne, tiny scones and finger food, canapes and napkins were assembled with love and care.

In the bright sunshine, Parker, Louise and her partner sat on a disused railway platform which fortunately was at the same height as my head and we laughed and drank our way through a much-needed lunch break. Other hikers threw us envious glances. Parker kept teasing them by raising his champagne glass.

I must share a long-standing, family fake, feud. Jay had lovingly bought Parker a resin replica of Donkey from the film *Shrek*, one of Parker's favourite films. It wasn't that I disliked this animal intrinsically but more that he just did not fit into my overall design scheme for any of our homes. Hence Parker would put him in the most prominent place within my display cabinet, amongst the Royal Doulton china. I would sneak up and place him on a lesser intrusive shelf on the other side of the kitchen, pinned with a note saying, 'Donkey's Stable!' Our adult children would hoot with laughter and side with Parker; how sad Donkey looked and would promptly find another eye-catching place to position him in.

This friendly sparring went on virtually right up until Parker's death. It became a family tradition as to who could outwit my Donkey manoeuvres. There was much leg-pulling and donkey play, if not horse-play, around the subject.

Unsurprisingly, I do not want to over linger on this year which was typified by weekly visits to the hospital, recovery from heart surgery, at the end of 2018, and the commencement of chemotherapy.

From the outset, Parker's oncologist was gently clear. His cancer was of a particularly aggressive nature but that they would try every option at their disposal.

Initially his chemotherapy was infused over three days from a jar that hung round his neck in a little pouch. He looked a little like a St. Bernard's guard dog. Incredibly, I was told that I had to undertake the sterile procedure to remove the jar from his stent line. I pointed out that I was extremely short sighted and flushing through tubes with syringes, which could endanger his life if incorrectly administered, was just impossible for me to do.

I did have one nervous attempt at it, being supervised by a friendly neighbour, who had been a senior theatre sister for over thirty years. She gently told me to stop, that she would take over. Even she initially struggled with the detailed instructions and the fiddly procedure. She thought it was nonsensical in this day and age that a layperson would be expected to carry out such a task.

This did little to salve my smarting pride, feeling that I had let Parker down because of my short-sightedness; that I could not do this important act of caring for him. He was very reluctant for me to sit with him whilst he was having chemotherapy and felt it was a waste of my time.

I began to feel excluded and rejected and I wanted the medical team to know that I was, in fact, a caring wife who needed to support her husband. His pride won the day until very near the end when I had to put my metaphoric foot down but more of that later.

Year 10: 20 March 2019

*The things that frighten us most are those that remind us
of our fragile existence.*
Sumiko Saulson

I had secretly done my research and I knew statistically only sixteen per cent of patients with stage four colorectal cancer survive longer than two and a half years. I was very gloomy then about the fate of the other eighty-six per cent.

I tried to make light of our wedding anniversary. We had bought cards for one another. Parker was a great one for cards. We sat close together in the lounge and with an uncharacteristic, solemn face he handed me a flat box, beautifully wrapped and said with a catch in his voice, 'I had intended to save this gift for our fifth wedding anniversary, but I think you should have it now.'

My eyes filled with tears and I tried to protest that he should save the gift for the next year but he was quietly insistent. On one of our many cruises we had visited a wonderful farm in Greece called Magna Gratia where we had spent a blissful day and had jointly bought a tiny, bronze olive tree.

It was a replica of a tree which had stood on the farm for a thousand years. In the magnificent jewellery shop, I had admired a lapis lazuli, Greek style jewellery, necklace and earrings. I took the lid off and gasped. A gentle smile spread across his face and he said, 'I knew you had fallen in love with it but you wouldn't allow us to spend so much money. So, I told you to go to the loo before we got on the coach and I nipped back and got it for you.'

This was one of the rare times that we held each other and cried and, without words, let go of our sorrow of all that was lost to us. The future was so uncertain. Somewhere he must have known, a deep and unconscious instinct.

It was not the happiest of anniversaries. Though we went out for a meal, his appetite was hugely affected by the chemotherapy. Everything tasted of metal and he had lost his zest for food.

On another fateful night, when he had just come back from having his chemotherapy, Parker insisted that he cook a pasta dinner. He said he felt fine and he knew I had been working all day. It was common for us to have a tussle as to who's turn it was to cook a meal as we both loved cooking.

Parker began to drain the spaghetti and did not notice that the thin plastic line to his chemo jar, round his neck, was melting in the hot steam. The next moment we had dangerous chemotherapy chemicals flying round the kitchen, over the dinner, over the floor, over the hot hob and work surfaces. This was the only time I ever saw Parker really panic. He ran to the sink and tried to stem the flow of liquid with his hands while I hurriedly rang the specialist, on-call nurse.

He had to drive thirty miles to Sheffield with everything wrapped in a towel. I had the hazardous job of clearing up the chemical spillage. There was a booklet literally written in red warning of the exposure to these chemicals. With mask, shoe coverings and inadequate apron I understood the first steps of pouring a neutralizing powder everywhere. It turned the chemo liquid into a jelly. It took nearly three and a half hours of anxious careful cleaning to get the kitchen as good as I could, made more difficult because I was in a wheelchair and the chemicals were going on my wheels. I then had to clean the chair.

I was, all the time, mindful that I was dangerously exposed to chemicals that could, in fact, cause cancer in me. I rang my sister-in-law for ongoing support whilst I undertook the procedure but it is true to say that I was harassed and not a little grumpy that Parker had got us into this mess because of his stubbornness.

I accordingly banned him from entering the kitchen whenever his jar was in place. As he did not demur, I think he understood that, on that occasion I too, had reached the end of my tether.

The cancer unit staff said that in all the years they had treated thousands of patients, they had never heard of such an occurrence. Parker had made local history in the unit!

24 – 26 May 2019

I tried to give some highlight to this year of treatment and decided to throw a surprise party for him. I secretly invited all his family and close friends for a weekend of frivolity to demonstrate our love by coming together.

The festivities were to begin on Friday night with a private dinner for his children, partners, brother and sister and the female cousin he was so desperately close to.

His face, when he saw Margaret, was something to behold. Sheer amazement, unfettered joy. He sat at the head of his table and took charge of the gathering as was his want. He said he had no idea that all this had been going on but, in truth, I'm pretty sure I had several slips of the tongue which I hurriedly tried to cover up. He must have wondered why I spent hours sorting out a playlist; which was not dissimilar to our wedding playlist.

I hired a retro singer who sang songs from the forties, fifties and sixties and she delivered her performance with panache and style.

I wonder, with all the gaiety, if I had made a miscalculation and Parker struggled with this gathering because he knew that they were aware that he was living on borrowed time. He could not bear any weakness to be displayed and I felt sad and regretful that my good intentions just may have gone awry.

One friend accused me of arranging his wake before his death and declared it was morbid. Such accusation hurt me profoundly as it was not my intention. We had always been party lovers.

Typically, of Parker, he refused to share with me what he really felt about that weekend or indeed display much gratitude for the enormous cost and planning involved. Perhaps he felt left out or overlooked. If so, I am sorry for it.

The next six months passed by in a blur of repeated hospital trips. By now he was suffering from anemia, due to internal bleeding, and he needed regular blood transfusions. He was so pale and listless much of the time. Moving from couch to bed with slowly increasing amounts of morphine.

October 2019

What is so poignant to tell is that Parker, with my encouragement, arranged a special weekend to go away with his three children and two grandchildren. I gently said to him that this was a very special time and perhaps he needed to think what needed to be said to the children as they might need to share with him poignant conversations.

I later discovered that Parker during the weekend exuded a buoyant charade of his old self, playing hide and seek with the grandchildren in the lounge and chatting nineteen to the dozen to the children about anything under the sun except his cancer. He and they were both in denial and, of course, I can understand why. He just wanted a happy time with them, like the old days but it left me sad because I hadn't seen him like this for months.

Within two months of this we had gone shopping for last minute Christmas bits and for some mad reason we decided we needed another turkey in case all the children dropped in. Parker had gone to load the car with the food while I nipped to the ladies. To my astonishment, there was a banging on the door and a woman was calling out my name. Parker was lying in the car park, amidst the freezing pouring rain and darkness. Several people kindly lifted him up. It was evident that something was wrong with one of his arms. The second type of chemotherapy he was now on left him extremely vulnerable to the cold.

A fantastic couple came to our aid, Pauline and Geoffrey. Ironically, they bore the same family name as my male siblings. Geoffrey was an ex-police constable and took charge of my car and all the shopping. I had to go and put it all in the fridge, lest it defrost, whilst Pauline took Parker to the local hospital; where he was diagnosed with a fractured humerus.

His cancer and the chemotherapy would delay and intensify the pain he felt from this fracture and to be helpless, unable to dress or undress himself, was a torture for him. I believe this was the beginning of the end. It was just one step too far for him to cope with and I noticed he began to eat less and less.

Year 11: January – March 2020

We are all so much together but we are all dying of loneliness.
Albert Schweitzer

Looking back now, from a stance of some months, it hits me with renewed force just what a truly dreadful two years we had struggled through. One terrible disaster of medical intervention for Parker who had always prided himself on being medically fit and strong.

Parker had been growing more and more distant over the last six months. He would just sit and stare at the TV blankly, or play 'Benedictus' on repeat which I guessed he was choosing for his funeral. At times it was hard not to scream at him and yell at YouTube simultaneously.

We were isolated in separate hells of misery. There were some rare moments when he would initiate some discussion but I had to choose any responses very carefully. It had taken me nearly two years to get Parker to make a Will. No-one would blame him for it. It is one thing to make a Will when one is fit and young but quite another when life looks foreshortened.

I spent most of the two years, that were supposed to be our dream retirement, alone in the double bed, for so many reasons. Parker felt better sitting in the lounge on the recliner. So many times I found myself crying silent tears in the kitchen with music playing to mask my own pain and terror.

I was now doing all the chores alongside travelling and working. One late night in February I arrived home exhausted. Saddened by his perfunctory hello, I was not paying sufficient heed and poured boiling water on to my leg, not for the first time either. I burst out wailing that it was all too much. I could not bear things anymore.

The only time Parker became emotional himself was when he overheard such distress. What a pity that we were not able to talk openly about our mutual sorrow, something I'd always believed was so important. Parker's defences were extremely strong. He just did not want to talk about his cancer and the prognosis. It was the same with his children. Jay would show his emotion on the phone which choked Parker up.

'Darling,' he would say, 'Oh darling don't cry I can't bear it.' I would wipe my eyes and apologise saying I was being silly. In truth I was being less than honest. My professional philosophy had always been the importance of helping people talk honestly about what was, potentially, going to happen. To help them to prepare for what they could not change and to change what they could; supporting patients and their families to make appropriate plans.

I couldn't seem to get through to Parker, the one man I cared about so deeply. Somehow it was much harder to talk to him about what really needed to be discussed. This made me very sad indeed. If it was at all possible to be any more miserable, I felt for the torture he must surely be going through himself; in the quiet hours when he could not sleep. He dreaded going to sleep and to bed and after an hour I would get up with him in the middle of the night to make him a drink. Sometimes he would sit on the edge of the bed and say, 'Life is shit, just shit.' This was the nearest he came to expressing his despair and outrage at all that had happened to him in the last two years.

There was never any talk about the future for me when he was gone or what his wishes were. In making a Will he began to reveal what his final wishes were, to be buried back in Brentwood.

Monday 24 February 2020

As we were dressing that morning we were both trying to act casually as if there was nothing different happening, just a normal, routine visit to the hospital to discuss the next round of chemotherapy.

In my heart I was very concerned because Parker would ask me, 'Do you think I am entering the last months of my life? I sometimes feel as if I am.' I said I didn't know and it was a question we needed to explore with the doctors.

My heart ached to see Parker struggle. He was such a proud man and to witness how he had been brought so dependent on others for care was so very sad.

I knew from personal experience how hard it was to let other people help. Parker struggled with small things like putting on his shoes and trousers. It was gut wrenching. To see this once proud man, who was always in control of everything and everybody, reduced to a shell, was a terrible tragedy.

9.00 am had sneaked up and we could avoid it no longer. I knew that today needed to be a meeting to really explore Parker's treatment plan. I understood that he could not bear feeling sick any longer. The pain combined with the constant taste of metal led to Parker making a unilateral decision to stop chemotherapy.

My nerves were stretched like elastic bands that were likely to snap at any moment under this mounting pressure. God only knew what he might be feeling. This appointment was a crucial one to receive Parker's scan results.

Doctor D was gentle but definite. The cancer was aggressive. It had grown even further in his bowel and there was some evidence of metastasis in the aortic canal, more numerous and enlarged. It had grown larger as well in the lymph nodes around the liver.

I knew the news was grave, emphasised by the cancer nurse taking my hands and squeezing them. Both professionals were compassionate but told us that the chemotherapy had not worked and, medically speaking, they had run out of options. The only thing left was to try immunotherapy in a different health authority.

My darling Parker turned towards me and asked me what he should do. My heart was pounding so much in my chest. I tried to keep my face looking calm and said that it had to be his choice but that it would be a long journey. I knew, from my research and work, that the side-effects were just as bad, if not worse, than chemotherapy, but I did not say so.

Almost in a rush he said, 'Let's go for that then, anything that might give me a bit longer.'

I took my courage in my hands and said to the consultant that Parker repeatedly asked me if he was in the last months of life. I said I felt it was not my place to try and answer these sorts of questions. The atmosphere in the room was burdened and pregnant with the weight of what I was saying I turned to Parker and held his hand.

The oncologist shifted in her seat and turned to Parker to ask him directly, 'Parker are you really, truly sure you want to know your prognosis, you really want to know the truth?' I was not surprised by his courage and determination as he sat up taller in his seat and said in a clear, decisive voice that he absolutely wanted to be put in the picture as he felt it was his right to know and make choices.

Then the hammer came down with the death sentence. Doctor D told him that without immunotherapy he had between three and six months to live but these were taken from statistics. The one thing she was categoric about was that there was no way back from this point. I tried so hard not to cry. I said I was desperate to go away for our fifth wedding anniversary and she said, 'Of course, we must try.'

As we had earlier agreed, I talked professional to professional, speaking about my concern relating to Parker's mental health and general deep depression which I did not think was helping his condition. She quite rightly pointed out that antidepressants would not change the reality of the cancer and the prognosis. I suggested that if they were sufficiently strong it might help with Parker's appetite and ability to fight physically a bit more. I went on to clarify that he had no quality of life; that he spent his days sleeping in a chair or bed.

Doctor D wondered whether he might just want to go home and be cared for and make the best use of what time he had. She gently said that there was no guarantee that another health authority, as an act of compassion, would assess him for immunotherapy. All she could do was make the request.

Given what had taken place, I asked her if she would complete a DS1500 form, which signified a patient has less than six months to live. She merely nodded and Parker bowed his head.

We slowly and silently rose to our feet and thanked them. The doctor nodded when she said she would try and get a referral for immunotherapy. I knew in my heart it was all too late.

The anti-depressants, he was later prescribed, were too mild and contained a sedative to help him sleep. All his poor body could do was sleep. We never saw the oncologist again.

I contend that from that day my sweetheart, literally gave up. My teddy bear of a man was eating a tiny bird portion of food on good days, no matter what I tried to tempt him with. I knew in my heart that the inevitable writing was on the wall. I tried to keep as cheerful as I could around him and kept suggesting that we might sing together or watch a film, all the things we would love to do, but he was too ill and too low.

All the deep love of Parker's children, his friends and my passionate love for my courageous darling Parker could not change what was to come.

Thursday 27 February 2020

The intervening days were filled with quiet strain, full of false smiles and uncertain reassurances. Parker wanted to know what I understood about immunotherapy. I was cautious in my replies because I did not want to place more pressure on him and prevaricated that he should explore this with the doctors in Nottingham. I did add, more truthfully, that from what I had researched, the possible side effects from it were as bad as chemotherapy which he had struggled with. He nodded and returned to his quiet contemplation.

Earlier in the week his morphine had once again been increased and he was even more sleepy and chair bound. Who could blame him?

I had gently, some weeks previous, suggested that the pain control was hopefully there to improve his quality of life and if he tried to walk a bit, his legs would regain some strength, as I'd noticed that they were wasting away.

I explained that if he just sat, the morphine would definitely make him sleepy all the time. It's such a narrow line to walk. What was support and encouragement with his condition? I was fearful that to someone with cancer, my words could be seen as crass nagging and uncompassionate.

I spent a lot of sleepless nights staring at the ceiling myself, fearful for the future. Let's be clear on one thing, you can have all the warning in the world, you may even fool yourself that you are beginning to prepare but nothing, absolutely nothing can prepare you for the reality of loss.

In writing this I am once again acutely aware of the many thousands of loved ones who have had to cope with absolutely no warning of the impending doom that Covid-19 was inflicting on their loved ones.

It is clear from the mountain of evidence and rapid research being facilitated in this country, as never before, that the scientists and doctors are still playing catch up with this menacing foe. To understand why this affects the elderly and ethnic groups more is of vital importance. The bereaved need to know as much information as possible to understand a bewildering, life changing loss. Why has this happened and why to them, in particular?

At least I have some rationale to understand why cancer, if not why stage four terminal cancer. Parker was definitely a man who lived life to the excess. He was sadly, probably, morbidly obese at twenty stone. He liked to pride himself that he was very fit and strong as he had played rugby and spent his life weight training. He would boast about his prowess in handling difficult arrests or going into a pub brawl to sort things out.

By the time I met him, at aged fifty-five, he had controlled Type II diabetes. In his youth he had been a heavy smoker but, to his credit, had given up this expensive, dangerous habit thirty-five years earlier. We might surmise that his earlier lifestyle and later complications may have predisposed him to cancer. Whatever the cause, the outcome was tragic and so difficult to accept.

Sunday 1 March 2020

I decided that I would not go back to work and leave Parker. I could not bear to part from my love. I quietly phoned my patients explaining that for the next couple of weeks I would have to speak to them on the phone.

Little did I know that the whole world would be caught in an unimaginable plague and that it would be, in fact, many months before I could speak to my patients face-to-face.

Parker insisted he was well enough, 'You should go to work.' Gently I responded that I wasn't prepared to leave him any longer. I needed to be with my dearest Parker now more than ever. He did not protest further. There were special afternoons when Parker would go to bed and I would climb into bed beside him and stroke his back very gently. He would sigh and say, 'Arh, that's so lovely darling.' It was like we were back again reliving our courtship.

I was profoundly aware that these moments were charged with such deep, wonderful, peaceful intimacy. We would fall asleep with our backs touching each other. I had to be very careful how I moved in bed because, at this time, the tumour had grown so large, and alongside his fractured arm, the slightest movement could exacerbate his agony. This was yet another reason why it was difficult for us to be together.

How I treasured those precious moments, even as they were happening. Tears film my eyes as I write these words and the memories burn inside me. This is my final tribute to a very special man.

In the days that followed I began to learn how Parker was pushing everybody away. Ariel, his eldest, gently told me that his three children had kept trying to reach their dad but he wouldn't answer his phone, which was very unlike him. I gathered this had been going on for some weeks and to a lesser extent for months.

Saturday 8 March 2020

I knew I'd made the right decision to stay at home as my darling Parker was deteriorating before my eyes. His morphine doses were increasing more and more under the guidance of his GP.

The continuing care coordinator and hospice occupational therapist had been in contact with us the previous two weeks. Although initially they tried to encourage Parker to come to coffee mornings and get support from other cancer sufferers, it was evident he was never going to do that. It was just not his style.

Parker was a very private and, in many ways, self-contained. He was comfortable with his own company. Before I met him, he would quite happily go for a two-week walking holiday on his own in the Peak District.

Thursday 12 March 2020

The day was grey and overcast. Parker was now so thin that I found it difficult to witness. I ceased mentioning about us going away for our fifth wedding anniversary. Parker told me, some weeks earlier, that he didn't have any clothes that fitted him any longer and I rather stupidly offered to buy him some new clothes. He looked so vulnerable slouched on the hall rocking chair.

The poignancy of the moment was not lost on me. Because of his fracture we cuddled awkwardly in silence; no words were necessary.

I knew in my heart it was hopeless and, I guess at some level, I had begun to collude with Parker. These unconscious defences, such as denial, can protect us from unbearable psychic pain; struggling to cope with the unthinkable approach of death and our inescapable mortality.

Over fifty-thousand patients and thousands of mourners would need such defences in the years and months ahead. Unlike my family, these victims of the cruel thief that was Covid-19 had no warning or preparation.

In the morning Parker struggled to walk to the bathroom to shower. Afterwards he barely made it back to bed, looking grey, breathless and very shaky. I knew things were moving on quickly now. His deterioration was rapidly increasing. There were moments when he was confused, whether because of the pain, the morphine or sheer terror, it was unclear.

By the evening I was completely at my wits end. Parker was crawling across the bed and crying out in pain for me to help him. He didn't seem to be able to comprehend that he must swallow his tablets and take his medicine to be pain-free. He was not able to make sense of it. An hour and a half later the tablets were eventually swallowed. It had been a terrible ordeal for us both.

Thank God for such good friends, June and Robert, who I had known for nearly forty years, were very supportive. Robert, a compassionate retired GP, listened attentively whilst I babbled out a torrent of distress. Parker was not eating et cetera. I asked him what should I do. Tearfully I admitted my and Parker's struggle. 'I can't get him to eat or drink or understand to take his medication.' Robert sensed my desperation and fear.

Despite all my years of caring for the terminally ill, I've never cared for a darling husband before who was dying. My dear friend reminded me that the only thing that mattered was to ease his pain, not to worry about food or water. I was to stop being so independent and ask for help. In truth, Parker and I were very similar, fiercely independent people. Robert told me to ring my GP and ask for the hospice to get more involved.

Friday 13 March 2020

The news was covering the anxiety, as the Covid-19 death toll climbed, and reporting the plight of our country. Italy was also reporting escalating cases. In the UK there was no mention of a lockdown at this stage but it was the topic of discussion on everyone's lips.

Instead I was focused on Parker's need for care. His GP was brilliant calling round within the hour of my phoning. Despite the unfolding crisis all around, she knelt by his bedside talking in a gentle, calm voice asking him what he wanted to do. We had in fact managed to discuss this in detail many months earlier and had agreed that I would keep him, if at all possible, at home in a place he loved. Under no circumstances, I promised, would he be admitted to a general hospital. Had Parker in fact gone to a hospital or hospice, we would not have been able to visit him and have the honour to care for him in his last days.

I arranged with the doctor and the hospice for a medical, ripple bed to be delivered to help forestall pressure sores. The district nurses and the hospice team were now involved. Parker spent the rest of the day in bed whilst I held his hand.

He was now deeply asleep for long hours at a time. The clock chiming precious seconds and minutes away seemed to symbolize to my exhausted mind the notion of our drawing ever closer to his end. If only I could have stopped all the clocks in the world and suspended time, I would have done so.

Thank God his youngest daughter Nicola came that evening to see him. Poor Nicola, she had worked all day and then had had a long train journey. I could see she was stunned and shocked at the deterioration of her father. Almost immediately we were engaged in Parker's needs. It took us nearly an hour and a half to get him to transfer from the bed to the wheelchair and then onto the special mattress in the lounge. It took us a further hour to persuade him to take his medication despite his great pain. He was so confused, poor darling, and anyone who has nursed and witnessed the effects of morphine will know what I mean when he kept saying, 'No more tablets.'

We decided to ask all the children to come down that weekend. They arrived the following day.

Saturday 14 March 2020

As I may have mentioned earlier, we always talked, with love, of our five children. We loved each other's children as our own and what fantastic children they were and still are. All the children had arrived by mid-afternoon on the Saturday and were joined shortly after by Parker's brother and sister. Thank goodness they were all there.

In the next twenty-four hours we all saw Parker in ever deepening confusion. In the early morning we caught him wandering in the corridor looking for the toilet. We were amazed he had got that far. The children helped him back to his bed but it was very distressing for them.

Parker's deep confusion persisted so I eventually rang the hospice and explored with them what was best to be done. A palliative specialist assessed Parker and recommended that it was time to put him on a morphine driver.

Even I did not realise how quickly he would become unconscious. I recall the bittersweet memory, shortly after the morphine started pumping into his body. Parker turned to me and with the sweetest smile said, 'Oh darling this is the best I have felt in months.' This is the last, lucid thing he said to me.

Whilst I've been focusing on the facts, words cannot do justice to this period. The sense of a dazed nightmarish feeling. Watching all this unfolding, witnessing the grief of the children, feeling helpless to adequately take away the terrible pain and cope with my own gut-wrenching sorrow.

At times, the hours took on a dreamlike quality, sitting by his bed and stroking his emaciated hand. Everything felt unreal as if it should be happening to someone else, not me, not us. But it was and we had to get on with it as best as we could.

Outwardly I was functioning, organising meals and caring for those around me whom I love so much. The external backdrop to all of this was the mounting anxiety of panic buying in the shops. We now had eight people to feed. I wanted to sit by Parker's bed for as long as possible.

We were all shocked at how quickly he seemed to slip away from us but we kept talking to him with the knowledge that hearing is the last thing to go.

On one poignant occasion, we played his favourite music 'Stranger on the Shore' and 'Danny Boy.' He started to sing and although it was weaker, his beautiful baritone voice echoed through the house. We were shocked to hear this spontaneous singing from Parker. Jay was standing at the door and we were both stunned. I broke down by Parker's bedside.

One of our retirement dreams was that one day we would sing in restaurants, as I have previously done. Parker roused himself and asked Jay to, 'Go and comfort Maria, she is distressed.' Then he promptly went back to sleep.

Our children were all fantastic pulling together, sharing the cooking and caring for Parker alongside me. I cannot praise them highly enough and it was the loveliest thing to see us all together in one apartment, small as it was.

Still, amidst our vigil, the growing disquiet of the outside world kept intruding. Parker's siblings reported the state of anxiety in the local hotel. Change was coming. The children came back with tales of shop queues of two and a half hours long.

One of the hardest things to bear during the next few days was the trauma of changing Parker's morphine driver at noon each day. Because of the general panic of patients ordering extra prescriptions, and the general need for morphine in hospitals, there was a worrying shortage.

Parker's brother, kindly and steadfastly, went from one chemist to another, ringing the GP trying to get the best drugs they could find for Parker. This was an issue that went on for the next nine days and was the source of continuous anxiety and frustration.

On one occasion, the wonderful district nurses sat for three hours waiting for this medication whilst various people from the hospice tried to locate the morphine. We were acutely aware of the pressure that these dedicated nurses were already under due to the pandemic. We felt so guilty taking up their staff's time. On the other hand, we wanted Parker not to be in any unnecessary pain.

What words can I say to explain. The vice-like grip, squeezing my heart as every day I watched Parker become more and more emaciated. By now he was only taking little amounts of water and we were gently reminded by the nursing staff that, at this stage, drinking could be dangerous for him as he could aspirate and choke on the liquid in his unconscious state. But I ask you, how could you leave somebody you love feeling thirsty and not being able to talk to you?

We moistened his lips by holding ice cubes up to his mouth. However, I worried constantly about his being potentially thirsty. This anxiety was heightened when Cam, my son, proudly announced he had made a mug of milk chocolate food supplement shake that Parker had been prescribed weeks earlier. Cam reported that Parker had drunk the lot and smacked his lips together in apparent satisfaction.

Sunday 15 March 2020

Parkers three children reluctantly had to go home. Ariel, the eldest, had two young children to care for; our adored grandchildren who were the darlings of both our hearts. We were indulgent and thrilled to be grandparents. Parker would love spending time with them. The children are a credit to their parents.

With apologies, I digress. Jay is a very compassionate and caring young man who works as an ambulance technician so had to return to work. My eldest daughter, Louise, steadfastly refused to leave me alone and was granted two weeks compassionate leave.

In the days that followed she cared for Parker with an empathy and deep compassion that took me by surprise. I began to think she was wasted working in a corporate company and wondered whether she should consider training to become a doctor. She found caring for Parker a moving and powerful experience. Never once did she complain about washing him, turning him and emptying his catheter bag. She was acutely aware that had Parker been conscious he would have detested being so helpless. The dedication she showed, combined with a tactful and natural manner, continually explaining in a chatty way exactly what she was doing all the time. These are skills that cannot be taught. I believe they are innate qualities. I could not be prouder of my daughter and I know if Parker were here, he would agree with me.

Thursday 19 March 2020

When all our attention was not focused on Parker, which was extremely rare, we were all watching the news and the Prime Minister's address to the nation about the grave challenges and sacrifices we would have to make in the selfless endeavour to protect the NHS and save lives.

Parker's three children were back with us by Thursday with news of the changes they had witnessed in the supermarkets and streets. Social distancing was beginning to enter everybody's mind.

We were all glad that Parker had been spared this additional major upheaval. Simultaneously we knew that if he was as well and fit as he used to be, he would have been among the first to volunteer to go back to the police force to help where he could.

One of us was constantly by his bedside, holding his hand, rubbing cream into his feet and heels, all the while chatting to him. I only wish Parker could have witnessed, in some ineffable way, just how much all the children loved him. It moved me profoundly to bear witness of their constancy and unflagging care. I know it would have made him so proud.

On two separate occasions there were powerful and poignant exchanges. When we were all gathered together in one room, I leaned forward and whispered in Parker's ear, 'Darling I want you to be at peace and know I will always love and look after our children. You can let go when you are ready, we will be all right.' You could have cut the atmosphere with a knife, the silence was humming in the room and suddenly Parker's eyes flew open and he said, in a loud voice, 'Aye?' We all burst out laughing with the release of tension as, clearly, he was telling us that he would go when he was ready and what was I babbling on about.

Secretly I was dreading the next day as it was to be our fifth wedding anniversary. I didn't quite know how I would get through it. I felt so broken inside.

On another occasion, a couple of days later, I heard Jay softly telling Parker, 'It's ok Dad, we will be ok, you can go.' My heart swelled with love and pride for him and his courage. Once again, Parker seemed to spring to life, his eyes opening wide and saying in a strong voice saying, 'Aye?' We all talked about it later and decided he was becoming more like his own father.

Friday 20 March 2020
Fifth Wedding Anniversary

The day dawned fairly sunny as I recall. The children had thoughtfully placed a table by Parker's bed, placing a big picture of the two of us. Alongside was a ubiquitous tissue box to hand as well.

To celebrate our fifth anniversary, I placed a piece of an olive tree, in the shape of a heart, into his hand. I knew that a fifth wedding anniversary is symbolised by something made of wood so I whispered softly, 'I love you my sweetheart.'

Through my flowing tears I told him that the heart symbolised our love. 'We are together on our fifth anniversary. Remember how we vowed we would be 105, in love together. Darling you have a good excuse.' I thought that, perhaps, I imagined a slight twitch of his lips into a grin. As I kissed him on the lips and repeated, 'I love you my darling,' and he replied, 'Love you too.' I tried to suppress my flowing tears.

Simultaneously I imagined him waking up and gently scoffing at my sentimentality. 'You will recall the wonderful day we spent on the tiny Greek island during our wedding honeymoon so it seemed an appropriate gift.' We had fallen in love under a bronze statue next to an olive tree. Sadly, all of this was possibly lost on Parker.

Later that day we sat and watched the beautiful wedding video that my daughter had marvellously, secretly created from numerous smart phones hidden around the room at our wedding reception.

The music was so important to Parker and myself as we relived such wonderful, happy moments. I remembered our combined joy. Softly I called to Parker, 'Darling all the children and I are enjoying the wedding video.' To our astonishment, he replied, 'I know, I am listening.'

Tuesday 24 March 2020

*The only time a goodbye is painful is when you know
you'll never say hello again.*
Author Unknown

*Sometimes I wish I'd never became so close to you that
way it wouldn't be so hard to say goodbye.*
Author Unknown

The morning dawned with heavy grey clouds that were a suitable metaphor for the leaden sorrow in our hearts. I had to tell the children that as Boris Johnson had declared legal lockdown, it was time for them to say their goodbyes and go back to their own homes. One can't begin to imagine the pain for these young adults of having to see their dad for the last time. I felt like I was some cruel enforcer.

Louise steadfastly refused to leave my side and would go into lockdown with me for as long as it took. Ariel had no choice, she had to get home to her two young children who needed their mother. Jay and Nicola had to return to their respective jobs.

Each spent as long as they needed with Parker though he was largely unconscious. I kept telling them that he could still hear them. I had to firmly tell Cam that, although he wanted to join his sister and stay with me, his dad might need help himself as he too was vulnerable.

Jay was very close to his father and depended on him for emotional and practical support. As he sat sobbing at his father's bedside, I laid my arms around his trembling shoulders. Like most young men he worked gainfully to put on a brave face and hide the devastation he displayed in every ounce of his being. I inadequately told him that he was to think of me, in the future, as Parker in a dress, that I would always be there for him and all the other children.

My dear, quiet son, Cam, said that he had not realised during Christmas 2019 that it would be the last one with his beloved stepdad. In different ways they all showed their quiet love and support for each other. Parkers brother and sister were also there.

We were caught together in time, in a small but luxurious apartment, in the Dudley village witnessing the end of an era. This end of an era was a cruel joke of fate as I had only known Parker for ten years.

Louise and I tactfully stayed out of the way, knowing we could have time to care for Parker afterwards. I guess we broke all lockdown rules as we held on to each other in the hallway. Saying goodbye felt momentously unbearable.

At last the apartment took on a quietness that had not been present for two weeks. The steadfast, hospice carer had called and invited Louise and I to wash Parker. We chatted to him all the time as we took care of all his physical needs. I was well aware that Parker now needed a quiet space and I had a strong instinct that now, with the children gone, he would begin to let go. I shared these feelings with Louise and the carer and we all agreed to leave Parker alone for a couple of hours.

Not being by his bedside felt torturous and the only way I could cope with this was to try and get the rest of the apartment in order. Up to eight people had been using the apartment for the last two weeks and things were generally chaotic.

Dusk was falling and, with fear in my heart, for some unknown reason, I opened the lounge door with trepidation. There was a different atmosphere inside, I could feel and smell it. My beloved Parker was going to a different place.

As I approached his bed, part of me was fearful that he had already gone but I heard him take a breath. I lit all the candles that I had in the apartment and placed them near his bed and I played music that I knew he loved. Louise, in the sweetest gesture, had found music by Enya that was gentle and soothing.

We both sat by his bed. I, whispered words of comfort to him as I stroked his hand and Louise gently stroked his feet.

There was a tranquility and calmness in the room. A gentleness, like the brushing of angel wings in the still air. 'Silent Night' began to play. It was a carol he loved so much that he had learned it all in German. He recounted that in the first world war that it was sung on Christmas day as men came together in humanity amidst the blood-shed. As I recalled this, I began to sing this carol to him over and over again. I smiled amidst my tears imagining he would open his eyes and say, 'Maria how many times are you going to enforce this on me?' He was such a joker and a man that adored life and laughter. Although his sense of humour, at times, could be cutting, you couldn't help but laugh.

We had sung 'The Prayer' as a duet many hundreds of times over and I sang my part to him now accompanied by Andrea Bocelli. It seemed so very fitting. Louise sat there with silent tears slipping down her face. We would stop to clutch hands or hold each other and she would occasionally go and make a cup of tea. It's amazing how calming and comforting tea can be, something from normal everyday life.

I knew that the Marie Curie nurse was coming at 9.00 pm to do an overnight sit with Parker. I felt very ambivalent about this because I did not want to leave his bedside, but the reality was that I had not slept for five nights. The children did not know this because they would force me to go to bed having sat with him through the day. I would wait until they fell asleep and would then tip toe to the lounge, stroke his forehead and hand. I felt he was afraid with the increasing breathing difficulties and irregular breathing. One literally sat on tender-hooks, wanting him to breath. It was a sign of heart failure that his big, bear heart was giving up.

I would bend over his bed as far as I could from my wheelchair making shushing noises and I do believe his breathing became calmer and even. He knew I was there telling him to relax. He knew he was not alone. Over and over again I must have repeated the same words for hours on end until my bones grew stiff and I was shivering with cold, despite my fleecy dressing gown.

The practical difficulty of this period was that three of his children were sleeping in the lounge where he lay so I had to whisper directly into his ear and make as little noise as possible. Furthermore, I was desperately afraid I might catch the bottom of their sleeping bag (or feet) in my wheelchair as I passed by. It made for hazardous driving.

They told me afterwards that they heard me all the time and that, more than once, I'd driven over Jay's toe! They're such great kids, so sensitive with my needing to be with him as I was for them. I can only say that I am so lucky to have such wonderful children in my life.

The Marie Curie nurse had been once before, two weeks earlier, and was disgusted that we had not had a night nurse in the intervening period. He was a tall, blond, no nonsense, Derbyshire male nurse with thirty-years' experience. He had a business-like manner saying a brief, 'Hello,' to Parker then checking all his paperwork.

He gave me a long professional appraisal under the rim of his spectacles and told me I looked like hell. 'When did you last sleep?' he asked. I remonstrated that I wanted to be with Parker but he gently told me that Parker could stay in this state for days, even weeks. My heart quailed at the thought, watching his meagre frame get smaller and smaller in the bed. Could I take much more?

To my utter astonishment the nurse turned to Parker and said, 'Now duckie your wife looks all done in and exhausted. I know you're used to being in charge and in control as a policeman but you have to let go now and give them a break.' I was horrified, 'You can't say that to him,' I protested, 'It's far too harsh and to the point. Anyway, I've already given him permission to let go and so has his son Jay.'

At those times you will recall, dear reader, he had opened his eyes suddenly and said, 'Aye!' as if to say, 'I'm not going before I'm ready, what are you talking about.'

The cancer nurse went on to explain that he had nursed many men, particularly young men like Parker and that internal rage kept them alive, longer than was good for anyone. I understood this analytically, but nevertheless I would never have addressed a patient in this way.

I knew Parker was angry about his dying, pushing away his children and talking to me less and less, not wanting to be held or cuddled, saying it hurt his stomach, but actually I think it hurt his love filled heart far more. He was retreating from us months before this period.

Reluctantly, I eventually agreed to go to bed at about 11.30 pm. Louise and I shared the bedroom and we both agreed we would not get any sleep that night as we had both had a premonition that tonight would be the night but exhaustion soon overcame us.

I jumped and was startled immediately; wide awake as the door opened. The nurse said, 'You had better come now and be with him.' An anxious fumbling of haste trying to climb onto my wheelchair as fast as I could proceeded. We drew alongside his bed and it was as if he'd heard us coming and was even now determined we should be spared from seeing too much. A long gentle drawn out sigh filled every corner of the room and we knew he was gone. I held him in my arms. He was still warm.

As I write these words I am sobbing uncontrollably. My body racked by the mere memory. I kept kissing him. Louise had her arms wrapped round me and we both kept clinging to each other in shock that this was actually happening.

Thursday 26 March 2020

Lives are like rivers: Eventually they go where they must.
Not where we want them to.
Richard Russo

In a daze, supported by my daughter, we went and registered Parker's death and began discussions with the funeral director about taking him back to the place where we'd been happiest for the first eight years of our relationship; the place he had called home for over forty years.

One of the rare conversations I'd managed to have with Parker was his wishes concerning what should happen after his death. He wanted to be buried in Brentwood. I asked Jay, Cam and Louise's partner and Nicola's partner whether they would be able to act as pall bearers for Parker's coffin. Although they were afraid and uncertain, all struggling with immense grief, they felt this was the last thing they could do for Parker.

Louise, my stalwart supporter in the days and weeks following Parker's death, was beside me twenty-four hours a day to offer care and love.

I nearly broke down completely when the funeral director asked me what I wanted Parker to be buried in. He was always such a smart, dapper man and although I nearly lost it, with Louise's help we found his favourite suit, matching tie, shirt and socks. Everything he would have wanted to be just so. As an ex-senior met police officer he would polish his shoes until you could see his face in them. I found his best ones.

When we are at our most vulnerable, dazed and confounded we are expected to rise to the challenge of a funeral made more difficult by the understandable restrictions. In our case we were more fortunate than so many as we were allowed ten people at his graveside.

The funeral was rushed with the undertaker explaining that they were worried about an avalanche of potential burials.

As we stood socially distanced, I dazedly watched as his sons and sons-in-law respectfully lifted and lowered Parker to his final resting place.

Because we were socially distant, we could not hug each other in our grief. However, we had a humane, female vicar who gave Parker a detailed eulogy from all the information I had given her.

Parker had requested that 'Benedictus' and 'Arvo Pärt - Spiegle um Spiegle' should be played at his funeral which we played at the beginning and at the end whilst his coffin was being lowered down.

Jay told me afterwards that lowering his father's body into the ground was one of the hardest things he would ever have to do in his life and his dad would have been the first person he would rush home to and say, 'You'll never believe what I had to do today,' and tell him all about it.

I think the music gave the proceedings dignity, solemnity and facilitated the shedding of some of our grief. Music is such a powerful force connecting us instantly to a well of deep emotions and memories associated with any particular piece of music.

It was a very chilly but bright March day. We had Parker laid to rest in a lovely spot near a path where I could park my scooter. After the funeral, because we could not linger, we quickly raised a glass of port, a drink he loved, as one more final toast to a very special human being.

Our children and grandchildren will surely remember this pandemic as a time of sacred upheaval, sacrifice and change.

In deciding to write this account I knew, as a psychoanalyst, that it is both potentially cathartic and simultaneously defensive. That I was trying to keep Parker with me alive in memory a little longer but, in so doing, work through the depth of grief and unspeakable sorrow I felt... so be it.

Some people might accuse me of this being a narcissistically, self-indulgent exposition of my own grief. I can see why this might be suggested but I know I have written it to try and show both his loved ones and, without sounding too grandiose, other bereaved people, that it is possible to use one's grief as a catalyst to help others.

About grief

I've written this book, up to now, and told you all the facts and details of how we met. The gradual falling in love, the fantastic marriage ceremony, the fun in the years that followed and the jokes we shared. It was not all sweetness and light, no marriage is. Even Parker could be irascible and pernickety at times and, of course, it got worse once the poor man was living with the reality of a terminal prognosis.

I was there and it was natural he had to share his rage with somebody. But that's what the vows are about. For better or worse, in sickness and in health. Although marriage might be going out of fashion, so we are commonly told, I believe most human beings want to be loved and give love. It's in our DNA and we need it like the oxygen we breathe. It's what kept us alive as newborn babies, the love of our parents for us.

You might ask yourself how can I tell the tale and seem so dispassionate. In truth, my grief is hidden in the gaps between every word a void between every line that I write. My grief is watered down to tiny tears shed for a few seconds in front of trusted family or friends but that is not the grief.

The grief, my grief, is like a stalking wolf constantly, stealthily circling around me, invisible by day and night. I try to pretend it's not there. I distract myself by food, by the television, chatting to friends and writing this book. Yet the grief I unconsciously evade, would not long be denied. My grief pounces in the dead of night and steals my breath away by the depth of my sadness and the flow of my lonely tears in the privacy of the darkness. My grief, my real sorrow, is cloaked by the dark, dark, night.

My anguish is carried away on the breeze as it whistles it's lamenting tune, the wind speeding on towards no particular destination. I can write this book because I know that besides the joy I had with Parker, my grief will never leave me. It might go underground for short periods of time, but, like all savage beasts, it will return unbidden, unexpectedly and with great stealth to wrap itself around my heart once again when I'm least prepared for it.

One can be the victim of such a predatory force, as long as one allows oneself to be, to collude with it and to hold onto the grief as a way of holding on to the one you love.

The simplified version, the theory of grief, is that we go through stages in order that we might undertake what might be commonly termed 'grief work.' The stages of grief typically include shock, denial, anger, searching and finally coming to a sense of resolution or acceptance. We take back the love we invested in that lost, departed person and in time we may reinvest this energy or profound attachment and emotion in another cause, human being or perhaps share it out amongst our loved ones.

This is the theory that, until now, with all the years I have worked with bereaved people I believed in and gave credence to. I like the hope that it contains. At the end of the day we can only hope that this hypothesis is true.

I hold to the theoretical understanding and hope of resolution not just for myself but for the many thousands of people around the world who have lost someone either through the pandemic or through other tragic causes such as cancer, ageing or all other forms of human frailty. Each grief will be unique to that person and their loved ones.

For the grief-stricken multitudes around the world, the form that sorrow takes will be different, not because they love less or because they love more. I believe the strongest instinct we possess as human beings is towards self-preservation and life which Freud termed 'The Eros Instinct.'

My hope is that the grief stricken will hold on to life around the world because, as human beings, we are unusually programmed to adapt to change. We have the ability to reinvent our realities and to find optimism and hope that drives us all towards life. Each day we live optimistically and believe in life. I know that life has to go on regardless of pain.

From the moment of our birth the one certainty enshrined in our life is that of death and yet most of us spend a lifetime trying to pretend that we are somehow immortal. We project this on to the people we love. Rationally, we know that one day they will die. That is our intellectual understanding that someday, we too, must end. Yet stubbornly we consciously remain with the illusion that they, with us, will go on forever, that nothing will change.

Somewhere, perhaps more in western civilization, we unconsciously collude with the illusion that death can be evaded and, along with it, grief and loss. In Victorian times, in Britain, society knew how to grieve. They wore outward symbols of sorrow; the drawn curtains as a funeral cortege passed by. The wearing of black or arm bands, for a prescribed period, proclaimed to the world that they were in mourning.

At this time mortality rates were so high that the reality of death could not be denied. They were reminded of its potential presence daily. With the advent of advancing medicine and technology, improved sanitation, diet and education, we have moved now to a place where such enactments of grief have become unfamiliar to us in Great Britain.

In this twenty-first century we have seen and have a growing trend in philosophy towards the body beautiful, as displayed in reality shows such as *Love Island* and *Naked Bodies*. Social media, the advent of Botox, facial lifts and tummy tucks are the new symbols of a denial of ageing and hence the social shrugging off of the notion of our impending mortality.

Sadly, social media and reality TV feed the lie to millions of people that what really counts is how we look on the outside; what designer labels we buy et cetera.

I say, in all humility, that what really matters is the beauty, the love that I hope we hold within us. I believe in this even through the grief. Although right now it feels as if the beast of pain that prowls around me will never be slain, I know one day that I will resume my life, pick up the pieces and the remnants of what was and go forward.

We all have to go forward into a path of not knowing where it might lead. We have to hold our heads up and find reasons to live; to laugh again. To love our children and partners, whether dead or alive.

We must talk about the loved ones that we have lost, not hide all their pictures away but use those memories to help us process and work through the unimaginable pain.

I humbly know that of the one-hundred thousand plus people that died alone in this country, not to mention the hundreds of thousands across the world, that no two ways of grieving will ever be alike. There is no blueprint or rulebook about how one should grieve or what one should do or indeed what might help, except I believe that talking to trusted people whether that be family or therapist, can bring comfort and strength. It is so often patients ask whether they are going mad. Overcome by despair they imagine they can hear, see or smell their loved ones. This is perfectly normal. It is part of the searching process for the one you have loved. It is not madness, it is grief in its rawest sense.

Despite all I've said above, I believe that we do grow in grief and pain. That we can use it to become stronger and wiser, more compassionate and more loving.

In ethnic cultures across the globe it seems to me that their diverse response to death is often much wiser. In Nigeria, they wear bright colours at funerals and celebrate the life lived. Within the Jewish culture they sit *Shiva* bearing witness to the loss of their loved ones. It is very important that we understand how faith and culture that is different to our own, impacts on the way a person will respond to the loss of a loved one.

I believe that there needs to be a national bereavement support scheme which can cater for diverse cultures and faiths by highly trained professionals in grief work and trauma. The current mental health provision in this country has been lamentably cut to the near bone and I do not think it will be sufficient to meet demand and the emotional fall-out from this pandemic.

It seems to me, in the end, that this is the best tribute I can give to my Parker. To become a better human being through the loss of him than ever I was loving him in life.

I know that each and every individual that has lost someone during this last terrible year will struggle towards their own solution, their own way of coping and sadly I know some may not cope and will need extra help and specialist input.

My heart aches for those people who knew that their loved ones were dying alone in an alien hospital environment. The courageous and skilled doctors and nurses would have done their utmost in unendurable circumstances to care with respect for their dying patients, but the loved one, left at home, could not sit by the bed, whisper words of love and comfort or hold their loved one's hand. What agony for them.

We must also consider the strain on front-line professional medics and the long- term, mental health needs of all staff working in the NHS and social care during this terrible year.

Having worked with bereaved parents and seen the horror and depth of their pain, when losing a child, these parents have lost their future; all the things they might have shared with their child as they grew to become an adult.

I have seen many parents who have turned their children's bedroom into a type of shrine. Toys and clothes frozen in time as if their little one has just walked out and will return at any moment. To help these people to begin to grieve is one of the greatest honours of my professional career. To draw alongside all those that are traumatised, is an honour that I take very seriously in all due humility.

Children too were lost in this pandemic. Siblings and parents alike have been snatched away, as well as partners. The care we extend to them, therefore, must be wide ranging and all inclusive, regardless of financial cost.

What I write here now will never come to the attention of the government or Boris Johnson, who has had a tragically marred leadership of this country. However, I intend to send him a copy and urge him, via a letter, for his government to think about the need for a highly professional, national bereavement service run by experts in trauma and loss. Sadly, I predict cases of pathological bereavement because people have not had the opportunity to say goodbye appropriately and to internally integrate the reality of death.

I know that many people might not ever get to see this book but it does not matter. The people that need to see it will see it and those people that want to read it will read it. It may mean nothing to most people and a lot to others. Parts of it will speak truth or comfort, whereas to some they might identify with a sentence or two.

A dear colleague and friend asked me why I was writing the book and I said, 'It was to help me "mark my grief" and if it was of use to anyone, then that would be an end in itself.'

I know I have written this account for all five children, their partners and Parker's grandchildren here today but especially for those grandchildren who will come afterwards. I want them to know who their grandfather was, what a loving, life enhancing personality, he possessed.

You are only really dead when the people around you, that knew you in life, stop remembering, stop talking about you. As long as you are spoken of or smiled about.

As the world braces itself for further spikes in the Covid-19 pandemic, we must reach deep inside ourselves to find wells of patience, compassion and selflessness.

I returned to face-to-face work with my patients in October 2020, socially distanced of course, and have volunteered to work with frontline workers who are experiencing emotional trauma or distress as a consequence of all they've seen and done. This is how my grief will be put to good use.

October 2020

On the 25th September, tomorrow as I write this, marks the six-month anniversary of Parker's passing. How timely then is it that I come nearly to the end of our story.

On the 9th October my Parker would have been sixty-five and as a family of six we will stand at his grave and honour him.

This is the memorial that I will place there on his birthday and what I will ultimately write on his grave stone:

My beloved Parker, on this your 65th birthday, 9th October 2020, I want you to know:
We will cherish the past and carry you with us in our hearts all the days of our life.
We will adorn the present with memories of you and the love you gave to all of us.
We will construct a future and you will always be a part of it in our souls, DNA and in every sweet thing you were.
Sleep well, you're ever loving, forever friend and wife, Maria xx

Graham
9 October 1955 – 25 March 2020

Acknowledgements

Above all, I wish to acknowledge the help and support given to me by my calm and humorous PA, Diane Davison, without whom this book could not have been typed. I wish to thank all my readers who have given me much-needed feedback on my initial drafts.

For those who may wish to read more about the issues discussed in this biography, the following books and papers might be of interest:

Mourning and Melancholia (1917) (1915 Volume 14 of the standard edition of the complete psychological works of Sigmund Freud) – published by Vintage Books London 2001 by the Hogarth Press and the Institute of Psychoanalysis.

Death in the Family by Lillie Pincus

Bereavement by Colin Murray Parkes

A Grief Observed by C.S. Lewis

Organisations that can offer some support to people who are bereaved:

The British Psychoanalytic Council – www.bpc.org.uk

The British Association for Counselling and Psychotherapy – www.bacp.co.uk

NB Only use accredited counsellors

Cruse Bereavement Care – www.cruse.org.uk

Age UK – www.ageuk.org.uk